AF540857

DPH Education Series

Management Education

P R TRIVEDI • K N SUDARSHAN

DISCOVERY PUBLISHING HOUSE
NEW DELHI-110002

Published by:

DISCOVERY PUBLISHING HOUSE PVT. LTD.
4383/4B, Ansari Road, Darya Ganj
New Delhi-110 002 (India)
Phone : +91-11-23279245; 23253475; 43596065
E-mail : discoverybooksindia@gmail.com
discoverypublishinghouse@gmail.com
namitwasan9@gmail.com
web : www.discoverypublishinggroup.com

First Published: **1996**

Reprinted: **2022**

ISBN: 978-81-7141-358-4

Management Education

Printed at:
Infinity Imaging Systems
Delhi

Preface

The *DPH Education Handbook* has been created to provide access to information about contemporary topics in education. Practitioners and students at all levels in education have a need to know what is happening today, in addition to historical treatments within the literature.

Each chapter within the Handbook is designed to provide the user with needed "state-of-the-art" information as well as further sources of information. One of the significant features of each chapter is the inclusion of specific programmes, projects and activities so that the researcher can locate human resources as well as the literature.

The handbook will be of use to graduate and post graduate students in education and to practicing teachers, administrators, librarians and planners. The chapters and the further sources of information cited in each book should lead the reader to thousands of people and documents for either research or programme planning purposes.

An effort to achieve universal and effective education is based on a recognition of the rights of students to basic education that enables them to thrive in a complex society, as well as a realization the technological and economic growth is facilitated by increasing the numbers of students, even those with poor academic progresses, who are, in fact successful in learning. Thus, recent and current efforts improve education serve both private and social interests.

This series is addressed to administrators, planners and educators working in the field of education and training with a view to stimulating interest and attention in the areas of education and its related fields. It is also addressed to a growing number of teachers and instructors who will be practitioners in education and who will need to be acquainted with the modern aspects of educational practice and development. Many ideas, generalisations and discussions presented in this series should also prove useful to employing organisations committed to provide training facilities within their establishments—leading to effective mutual participation by institutions and organisations.

The editors wishes to thank the contributors, as well as those organizations that gave permission to publish their extracts, chapters etc.

Editors

Contents

1 Management Theory and Education

Management theory and education

There are many misconceptions about management. It is often thought that management is a precise technique or collection of techniques that can be applied to almost any situation with the consequence of immediate improvement. But the word 'management' is no more exact than the word 'organise' or even the word 'teach', though it is a generally useful word to describe the activities necessary to influence control, direct or influence people who have come together with a common purpose. While it is true that there is a great deal written and spoken about management 'techniques', techniques are aids to management not the whole of management itself. It is certainly a delusion to believe that one can be taught techniques that will ensure immediate effectiveness in situation that require management. Indeed, one of the great disservices of 'management education' has been the formulation of the idea that there is an exact science of management that can be learned like engineering or botany or computer programming. An even more unfortunate development has been a rise in expectations that management 'techniques' from one area can be applied in essentially the same way to other situation. The idea of 'education management' often suffers from this misconception so it is important for us to try to understand what exactly management means in the context of education.

Management "theory" is rationalisation about management activity. That is to say, a manager or management 'thinker' reflects on his experience and attempts to make sense or it. He interprets what he has seen or experienced and attempts to make valid generalisations from it. In making generalisations or hypotheses he begins to develop a theory of management. If he interprets his experience of management as strong, firm leadership, then he will derive a theory of strong firm leadership as a key concept in his idea of management. Most management ideas are pragmatic in this sense and are interpretations of experience. Other managers have different experiences and express their theories differently. Most management theory is subjective because it focuses on the practicalities of bosses getting other people to work for them and develops around personal preferences in behaviour. My own view of management theory is not intended to be cynical but rather to be realistic. Managers tend to need answers quickly and to live lives characterised by considerable urgency. They make decisions intuitively and forthrightly because they are usually under great pressure from a wide range of other people. We are still in an age when managers like to listen to other managers till how they do things and they often justify what they do by the 'results', almost always quantifiable matters.

Management is a comparatively recent concept, just about one hundred years old. It has been invariably been associated with commercial necessity and financial investment, and only since the second world war has the idea of 'management' been extended to other areas of human activity and organisation. There is still a considerable confusion about management as a commercial toll and management as a concept of organisation. Yet we should more properly apply ourselves to the understanding of organisation, because management is an aspect of organisation. Techniques of management tend to be technical instruments and procedures but the use of techniques depends on an understanding of the nature of organisation. Increasingly the understanding of management is coming to depend on an understanding of how people behave in organisations. Techniques fall into place when we understand how they relate to people but the understanding of people must be the first concern. Banks and railways could be entirely automated but management would still have to concern itself with the people who use banks and railways, the technologists could do what they like to the systems but without being concerned with people, they would not be managers. Managers, then, are people who deal with people in organisations and we must understand how organisation function if we are to understand management.

In education, there is very little technology but a good deal of human organisation. In essence, education is a relationship between a teacher and a learner. Learning can be machanised in various ways but by and large education is generally recognised as an interpersonal activity. One runs schools with people not machines. However may mechanical aids to learning there may be, people are always paramount so if we talk of management in education, we are almost entirely concerned with people. In this respect, education is a good model for management because since it has only a peripheral commercial purpose it presents us very clearly with problems of interpersonal relationships or human organisation that are obscures in so many other cases.

The basis for a theory of management should properly be a theory of organisation. Doubtless organisation theory is no less subjective than theory of management but it is of a different order. If management theory is in all likelihood an expression of personal preference about how managers ought to behave, organisation theory is a reflecting on how people are perceived to behave. So organisation theory is an aspect of social psychology - the behaviour of people in organisations. Organisation theory is descriptive of how people behave collectively and predictive of how they are likely to behave when formally organised. Formal organisation is simply a pattern of behaviour constant over a period of time and repeated in some way. A bus queue, by this definition, would be formal behaviour but it would not become organisational until someone began to influence the behaviour of the people in the queue. Once influence is exerted on or within a group, formal organisation occurs in predictable patterns - or at least in patterns which could have been predicted though they seldom are entirely predictable in practice.

Management theory tends to assume a greater degree of prediction than actually occurs. Since management is about control, the best theory will lead to greatest prediction and most control. At a low level prediction is often accurate but in critical situations, prediction is a matter of open choice. Organisation theory is less concerned with prediction than exploration though as a consequence its predictions are greater. Organisation theory is not concerned only with overt and superficial behaviour but also with psychological reasons and motives. Perhaps at this point the destinction between management theory and organisation theory becomes blurred but it is important only to realise that what concerns us is the reality of organisational behaviour rather than the deception about what goes on when people organise themselves.

While organisations are 'objective' in that certain key characteristics can be generally agreed-location, size, numbers of people concerned-the ways in which we understand them are quite subjective. This is one of the basic problems of organisation theory. However much we may be able to describe objectively an organisation, each of the members will perceive what is going on quite subjectively. It is because of the multiplicity of subjective perceptions of the organisation that 'management' is such a problematical but exciting activity. We must use certain therms to describe an organisation and there has grown up an important vocabulary of organisation theory, but once we have learned to use the terms, we have to subject them to scrutiny to discover the meaning of the organisation to each member for whom a given issue is critical.

All organisations have structure but 'structure' is only a description of what happens in the organisation; it is not a separate entity so there cannot be imposed a structure on an organisation. We can, however, bring about changes in behaviour and as behaviour becomes characteristically patterned we observe characterstic structure. Labels on people in an organisation tell us very little about how they behave, though they may tell us how they are 'expected' to behave. Understanding the nature of organisational structure is often the biggest problem for newcomers to organisation theory because they cannot understand how structure can be so fluid. Yet the essential characteristic of organisation is fluidity or its 'organic' quality. Just how fluid an organisation is depends on how control is exerted and the amount of freedom members feel themselves able to exercise. There is always more freedom of structure in an organisation then members ever realise and the work of consultants is frequently with increasing the amount of permitted movement in the organisation.

The drawing up of organisation charts is more often than not a method of control than a description of real relationships. In the same way, job descriptions are more often prescriptive than liberating. Good management should be concerned with freeing up the personal energy in an organisation since the more energy available the more the organisation can grow and develop but often managers want to limit freedom for economic as well as personal reasons. For educational institutions there is a real issue between whether more freedom can be given or more control and direction imposed. On the whole, educational institutions do not encourage a great deal of creativity but are more concerned to regulate closely the behaviour of the members towards certain clear but limited goals-examinations.

Though we may think of organisations as impersonal entities - the word 'institution' implies this - they are in fact 'collectives'. That is, they consist of people engaged in collective activity. This being so, organisations can hardly be said to have goals though their members may do so. It is better, therefore, to think of organisations as serving purposes for the members and for goals to be objectives which individuals agree to pursue for personal and individual ends, or to gratify certain personal needs. It is important to understand that the only goals are personal ones and that no one's personal needs can arbitrarily override anothers. Sometimes, bosses or other individuals objectify their personal needs into organisations needs and, perhaps more often, personalise organisational needs so that organisational and personal needs are seen to coincide. But a boss cannot say that his personal needs and those of the organisation are identical without exerting excessive influence over his colleagues. The exercise of authority within organisations is a major critical aspect of organisational dynamics for it is always difficult to determine just how legitimate the exercise of authority by any individual or group may be over others. Managers are inclined to assume that they have greater authority than they in fact have. That they always have less than they believes is evidenced by the crises faced by organisations when decisions are not fully implemented.

The dynamics of organisations can best be understood by observing the dynamics of small groups. There is an extensive literature on group dynamics which has produced a valuable vocabulary. Already we have used the terms structure, membership and authority; others will be introduced as we proceed. Organisations are very difficult and subtle phenomena to understand. It is impossible to understand everything that is happening in a large organisation like a school or college by simply observing; the essential dynamics are beyond observation. But we can use our experience of small groups to create personal models of organisation and from these we can extrapolate to larger institutions. These organisation models are psycho-sociological in that they derive from an understanding of the psychological relationships between group members and the way issues and problems in the group are realised and dealt with. The dynamics of a group and organisation are the processes by which the various tasks of the group are accomplished. It is customary to speak of 'process' as the description of how groups behave and 'task' or 'content' as what these groups attempt to achieve. Since dynamics are by definition fluid and changing by description of an organisation can be no more than a snap-shot picture of what was going on; changes between the moment of analysis and the present may be very considerable indeed.

Change is characteristic of organisations; that is to say, it is in the nature of organisations for them to be constantly changing. Though may try to impose specific kinds of change on an organisation, or seek to bring about certain changes within an organisation, change is a constant reality and there is no means of knowing what is or is not a 'natural' change. On the other hand, it does seen likely that there are certain changes that are 'more natural than others' - that is, changes that would occur if there were no conscious or deliberate efforts to bring about change. One of these natural tendencies is towards break up since all organisations break up eventually. Another change is away from one kind of order towards another. Since all conscious management effort is aimed at order and the continuance of the organisation organisations will experience the tension between break up and order. It seems probable that many organisations are kept in existence long after they have ceased to serve their most useful purposes.

Utility is another important idea in organisation theory. If people engage in purposeful activity - and for the most part this is what they seem to do - then organisations have continually to serve useful purposes. Thus usefulness will be variously and subjectively judged but it can be assumed that members require consciously or unconsciously to get something out of their membership. That 'No one is in it for nothing' is a useful maxim if we are to fully understand organisational behaviour. Each individual is in the organisation in expectation of a 'return' for his membership - for some form of social and psychological exchange. In organisational terms there is no such thing as pure altruism; altruism is imply a mutual self interest. To look at organisational membership in this way is itself useful and enlightening for it enables us to explain a good deal that is puzzling about why people join, and especially remain in, an organisation. So far a educational institutions are concerned this is a useful way of understanding the teaching/learning relationship and of uncovering the kinds of satisfactions that membership gives.

It is axiomatic that no two individuals perceive an organisation in precisely the same way. We view everything in the light of our experience. That means we perceive the reality in organisations differently and interpret events accordingly. We all have experience of 'good' and 'bad' days which do not coincide with other people's 'good' and 'bad' days so that one is jaundiced while another is euphoric and vice versa. One way of understanding these different perceptions is to view them as fantasies. We each have our fantasies about an organisation to which we belong and interpret what we see and experience in terms of our fantasies. Where the fantasies of different people are compatible or congruent no problems arise, but where they are incompatible considerable difficulties can ensue. Irreconcilable differences between people arise because they cannot understand the nature of one another's fantasies, indeed are often totally unaware of them. This theory parity explains differences that disorientate people by finding the atmosphere of an organisation just simply uncongenial, unsympathetic or discomfiting.

Each organisation develops its own culture or ethos. That is to say there is a prevalent system of values, customs and mores which are peculiar to and characteristic of that organisation. In schools, terms such as 'ethos' or 'tone' may be used and they refer to what is generally though to be indefinable but characteristic. In reality, it is much less undefinable than inmates often assume because it is possible to discover dominant values and behaviours be careful observation and discussion. The 'feel' or 'ambience' of a place is essentially a consequence of behaviour patterns which in turn derive from personal attitudes and values. These become manifest in quite tangible matters, events, procedures and behaviours which are so taken for granted by members that they fail to see them and recognise their significance.

There are, of course, a lot of matters not obvious to the onlooker, but an experienced and perceptive onlooker can see a long way behind the superficialities. Human intuition is much more active than many are ready to concede. Much of our training and education is to detach ourselves from natural sensitivities yet we can only ever come to understand organisations when our natural senses have been re-educated.

Understanding organisations is not a magical or esoteric skill. It is a necessity for all of us because we spend most of our life in organisations of one sort of another. Membership demands survival but more than that an awareness of ourself as a member is vital if the usefulness rather than the destructiveness of organisations is to be experienced by us. All too many organisations are places of misses opportunities, lost battles, frustrating experiences, pious and unrealistic hopes. With understanding they can be a means of personal enrichment.

The dichotomy in management is always between the interests and needs of the individual against those of the organisation, though in practice this means the needs of one individual against the needs of another. As we have seen, there is no such thing as an objective organisation only one that is identified in various ways with various people. Depersonalising organisations is the great fallacy of management theory and one of the destructive errors of organisation thinking. Always in organisations the interests of one individual are being brought against the interest of another and the conflict is furthered by colluding into group issues. Since all relationship involves some form of bargaining and all bargaining is a form of conflict, it follows that organisatins are arenas of conflict. We might even say that conflict is the latent dynamics of organisations. As we resolve conflict, so organisational activity takes place. When it is resolved in the best interest of all those involved, the organisation is healthy; when the resolution is one sided there is trouble Few organisations have mechanisms for the satisfactory resolution of conflict and so trouble arises. Much management thinking aims to avoid conflict and that is a major error. Conflict avoidance and consequent flight from the real issues puts an organisation into a cannot go on and anxiety and frustration ensue. Conflict resolution must be mutually acceptable if it is to be fruitful to the organisation and so solutions that are the result of managerial coercion are dysfunctional.

Organisations are replete with rewards and punishments, part of the psychological exchange that must go on. When rewarding and punishing is arrogated to a manager the potential for unresolved conflict increases. Provided a manager is perceived to be a genuine 'third party' in conflict resolution, he can serve a useful purpose as arbiter, facilitator or umpire but where he is seen as arbiter by authority of his position rather than his personal position as a member, then problems of great seriousness arise for he exercises personal judgements and preferences in line with his own selfish needs and increases his coercive power over other members. That this is what happens in organisations is the greatest pity; a consequence of our social attitudes towards power control and authority but in terms of pure organisation theory no one can take unto himself, or be given by an outside agent, power over members that does not derive from his relationships with those members, without dire consequences. It is these dire consequences that are at the root of many organisational problems that we have to deal with day by day.

Within the organisation, each person has a position, or rather a number of positions, in which he relates to other members. In organisational terms these positions are called 'roles', a role being the behaviours associated with a position in terms of the interactions among people in the organisation. Every member of an organisation by virtue of his membership has a position, and role behaviour develops as a simple consequence of the passage of time. Usually titles or names are given to roles in the expectation that the role incumbant will follow a traditional pattern of behaviour generally associated with that role. But the functions of his role do not belong to the title but to the organisation. It is no use calling a leader of a climbing party a secretary and expecting him to type letters instead of leading a climb, and this is true of all roles; roles are determines by organisational needs not by designations. Around roles are expectations, the way other members expect roles to be worked out and fulfilled. None of the expectations exactly coincide so there will always be discrepancies between expectation and fulfilment as well as different expectations. When the differences are significant, there arise critical issues for the 'organisation'. Most people fall back on what they believe ought to be appropriate role behaviour without trying to find out what has happened, why it has happened and how it may better fit into the reality of organisational behaviour rather than hypothetical expectation.

Behaviour in organisations occurs for the most part in groups or in relation to groups. Organisations may be considered a federation or coalition of groups. It has been suggested that educational institutions like universities are loosely bound groups while schools consist of tightly bound groups. Sometimes the importance of groups over-shadows the importance of individuals yet individuals come before groups. Each individual enters an organisation as a person in his own right with a whole idiosyncratic range of needs and talents,. a distinct personality. Managers often forget the importance of individuality perhaps because it is easier to deal with objects rather than real flesh and blood people. Personality, too, as a concept is very difficult to handle because there are so many approaches to understanding personality. We can however be clear about two things. Each individual will behave fairly consistently and true to type and he will be somewhere between being an authoritarian and/or dependent person and being collaborative and/or autonomous. By and large we can be fairly certain that however we interpret an individual, his behaviour will be consistent in personality terms and in terms of organisational behaviour. If this were not so, interpersonal relations would be virtually impossible. It is these two truths about individuals that make organisation analysis possible.

A useful theory of personality and organisation that blends an explanation of personality theory and organisation theory derives from a scheme proposed by O.J. Harvey. It suggests four stages of personal development and four stages of group or organisation development. These stages are dependence, counter dependence, interdependence and independence. The usefulness of this idea - which sounds naive as related here in bald terms - is that it suggests how personality and organisational culture or climate match or mismatch. An individual who is psychologically dependent will feel most at home in an organisation that creates dependency by having strong autocratic or paternalistic leaders, likewise with other phases. The important idea arising from the theory is that when we look at people in organisations we should always be looking for matches and mismatches between individuals and organisational climate. We can do this with whatever theory of personality we may prefer, for example the Jungian theory of type or Personal Construct theory. Detailed analysis can only be made by a careful study of people as persons and organisations as cultures.

Organisations do not remain static, in the same state. The inherent tendency to change has already been mentioned but there are phases of development that are important to our understanding. Organisations have a starting up phase during which new members are recruited and certain routines and practices are laid down. This is followed by a consolidation phase in which there may or may not be a significant change in membership. After this comes a period of stability and then some form of expansion or renewal. Periods of quiescence and activity alternate from then onwards until the organisations closes down. These phases can be predicted only with the grossest generalisation but what does appear incontrovertible is that organisations do pass through phases of development and that these phases require different kinds of responses from members. The kind of boss who is happy in a period of expansion and novelty will quite probably be unhappy during a period of consolidation. Similarly, a member who functions will during a period that requires much routine work will be unhappy when he is required to change his style towards entrepreneurship so that the organisation can grow. It may well be that leaders should be changed for various phases and some mechanisms will have to be devised to assist them to take on different roles.

Related to the development of organisations, in the sense of their changing nature, is the concept of career. Organisations are locations during the career of an individual it is not possible to pursue a career without being involved with organisations, at least at essential points. An individual will usually be a member of several schools or colleges during his professional career as a teacher. He will look on each institution as a place where his current career needs can be fulfilled and these needs will change from institution to institution. There is another example of the need to match individuals and organisations. Organisation needs arise from the needs of the people in the organisation; they require help and assistance from someone else whom they seek to recruit. An individual looking for a new job may be very conscious of the need for promotion but he will be dissatisfied with promotion alone. Status may not be enough, certainly not for a long period of time. What he will be looking for are opportunities to use his skills and talents and to feel a part of the organisation; that is, one of a group of people with congruent interests and work styles. There can be nothing impersonal about an organisation; often the quality of material surroundings has low significance measured against a feeling of happiness or contentment. Recruitment is an essential part of organisational functioning and members need to be exceedingly careful about how it is done. The idea of career is often interpreted as promotion but that can only be a part of the story since not everyone can reach the top. If not being 'promoted' is seen as a condemnation or punishment then we are in a highly judgmental situation. Organisations cannot function with everyone at the top and it would appear unquestionable that all members are some kind of 'equal' importance. The belief that only the people at the top are important hardly bears examination yet it is one of those myths that it is difficult to discount. Careers are about finding places where an individual can find most personal fulfilment and this may or may not involve adultation by others. The mistake so often made by mid-range members is to denigrate the importance of their junior colleagues. Perhaps it is significant that it is impossible to find language to describe locations in an organisation that is not hierarchical and often judgemental. The problems of hierarchy in organisations are ones that we shall return to time and again because status seems to be preoccupation with members of our society at large.

It is comparatively easy to outline the vocabulary of organisation theory and it is not very difficult to understand because most of the words and phrases come from ordinary speech even if the social psychologist does make something of a jargon of them. Applying the terms to specific organisations is a little more difficult because our experience of any organisation is so overlaid with our whole social experience. Even until quite recently many teachers rejected the whole idea of management applied to education as being totally outside their experience of what was needed in education. As interest in education management grew it resulted in an attempt to foist industrial; and commercial techniques onto education - usually with little understanding of either industry or education. More recently interest in organisation theory rather than management "theory" has frown up as has been indicated in earlier part of this chapter. So the best way of understanding an organisation is simply in terms of our experience of it rather than in terms of how we think an organisation should be organisation should be organised. Obviously our experience of a small primary school is different from that of a large polytechnic.

An issue that has preoccupied many people is that of the size of the institution. It is held that the most critical factor in differentiating among organisations is the factor of size. That is, significant features are a function of the size of the organisation. This is only partly true because size is not itself a uniform matter. A polytechnic with 7,000 students on a single campus is different from a polytechnic with 7,000 students on ten campuses. Only some management functions have universal applicability throughout the institution. Furthermore, is a primary school of 200 children a single institution or is it one campus of primary education in a Local Education Authority of seven thousand primary school children? Here is the key to understanding organisations. Whatever the size of the organisation, activity will occur effectively in smaller units and these units will be social units of five or six people. Of course, administrative demands may be on a larger scale and the effect of bureaucratic procedures will be to enforce delays, but it does not seem to follow that overall large units are more effective or efficient than small units *per se* and the reverse is equally true. Although there is a suggestion that very large units are inefficient it has yet to be satisfactorily demonstrated firstly that large institutions are either better or worse than small ones and secondly that small institutions have any advantage over large ones. Because an individual has a certain kind of experience of a certain type of organisation it does not follow that everyone else will have the same experience. While it is the individual experience that is important, we must be careful not to extrapolate to a broad generalisation from one experience. Education is bedevilled by complete lack of research into the effects of size but there are many untested assumptions. Every educational institution will have membership, location, times of working and will be embedded in a socio-economic environment. It will provided a distinctive experience for everyone who comes into membership, however brief that period of membership may be, and in describing that experience we experience we describe something of the culture of the institution, an experience of the ethos. It is probably more important, pragmatically, to understand how one comes to experience an institution in a certain way than to be able to analysis statistically what goes to make up an institution. Most analyses with which we will be familiar are of the quantitative, statistical type and they tell us very little unless we want to make financial decisions. We need to know more than that the size of the English Department is 10 teachers, four of whom are part-time and six women with a head of department who is aged 38. We soon become interested in the personalities of the people in the department and how they interact. We become interested in the role of the married women and how their careers develop around their growing children. We note that the Head of Department is keen on promotion to a Headship and is trying to gain favour to be promoted so second deputy of the school. We discover that three of the departments want to teach drama and communication skills while two continually regret the days of formal grammar. These kinds of behaviour and relationships are what organisation theory is all about. They explain motivation, commitment, ambition, leadership style. alienation, disgruntlement and so on - all the behaviours that are the subject matter of social psychology. To describe educational institutions in these terms is to make an analysis of use to the task of managing the organisation.

The task of management is to facilitate the development of the organisation. Earlier management was described somewhat pejoratively as control. That is true but control may be authoritarian and judgemental or facilitative and accepting. Managers are required to make decisions by virtue of their positions but how they make those decisions is a matter of their choice.

Because organisations exist only for the people who are their members - that is, in practice organisations can perform only what their members are willing and able to perform - it is important for members to have a genuine feeling of being part of the organisation, or rather as much a part as they feel the need to be. The job of the manager is to mediate among the various demands made and the various kinds of commitment members and clients will give. He does this in situations such as that of the English Department described above. Each distinct group of members has a distinct range of demands, commitments and contributions.

In education - as in hospitals and other service organisations - there are two groups of membership. All organisations have members and clients or customers but in education there are at least two groups of members and at least two groups of customer. The members are teachers and students who have different career needs in the school. The customers, or clients, are the parents of pupils and the 'consumer' or employer of the pupils when they leave. It is better to think of employers as part of the general environment in which the school must function as a socio-economic entity. Employers as a group are no more unified or real than society at large and in some ways too much credence is given to what some employers say at a given time. Employment prospects are much wider than many employees are able to envisage. Parents, however, do have a special relationship to the school since the task of education that the school performs is on behalf of the parents. The student however is neither customer nor even client. He is a full member of the school although there is some differentiation of function. Exactly how this function is perceived will depend on the philosophy of education of the perceiver. If we see learning as a partnership we shall have one view of educational organisation (structure) different from those who see teaching a s didactic relationship. Perhaps increasingly teaching is coming to be seen as a two way relationship and this is certainly so in Higher and Further Education. Hence the organisation of teaching will depend on the philosophy of education of the heads and teachers; it will be an expression of their understanding of the educational relationship.

However large the educational institution, the primary task will always - by definition - be teaching. Management has not other purpose than to facilitate this activity. Since no human activity is organisationally simpler than that between a teacher and his student, the more complex educational organisations become, the less likely they are to fulfil their function.

2 Management Education Skills

The collection of techniques covered in this text forms part of what is known as the discipline of Operations Research, Management Science, or decision Science. For the remainder of the text these terms will be used interchangeably. They all imply the same context: analytical techniques that *aid* in the decision making process. From its very inception in military operations to present-day industrial, service, government, and social applications, the common thread throughout the development of operations research has been its relevance to decision making. When looking at the various components of Operations Research, however, one is sure to see that each of these components of Operations research, however, one is sure to see that each of these components has become a mini-discipline of its own. As a result Operations Research/Management Science/ Decision Science is often viewed as a rather loosely connected collection of theoretical techniques.

While it is certainly true that each of the techniques has developed its own identity in terms of a body of theory and applications, their common use is that of an aid to decision making. The aim of our text is to uncover the underlying thread of an aid to decision making. While this is our ultimate goal, it is necessary that the techniques be presented individually so that the underlying principles of each can be understood. while there have been numerous successful applications of these techniques, almost every application presents some aspects not apparent in other applications. The decision maker who is well founded in the basic concepts of the techniques is better able to propose, apply, and modify the techniques to fit the problem that he faces. One must not change the problem to fit the techniques; rather, one must modify the technique to fit the problem.

Seeing some real applications of these techniques can greatly benefit the reader; therefore, we have included numerous examples. The examples take three forms; example problems and their extensions presented in the text; an extensive set of references at the end of each chapter listing readily accessible applications; and finally, a chapter that uses some cases of real applications as a teaching exercise.

The concept that is used to tie together the complex decision making environment and the OR techniques is that of a *model. A model is some representation of a real-world phenomenon in a structure simpler than the original structure of the phenomenon.* Models are in general of two types: *physical* and *conceptual*. The idea of a physical model is well known to all of us - model airplanes, ships, and cars represent scaled-down versions of the "real thing." Physical models are often used to test the design of a component of a complex system without involving or endangering the entire system - for example, wind-tunnel tests of models of airplane wings or rockets. It is clear that if the results of testing and experimenting with physical models are to be of practical significance they must accurately represent the full-size end product.

Our concern here will be with conceptual models - abstract representations of decision making processes. We have been exposed to and have utilized this kind of models in our everyday experiences, too; for instance, the use of road maps in planning a trip.

These conceptual models are abstractions of the actual decision making situations and represent a formalized means of evaluating alternative courses of action. One of the major characteristics of modern decision making processes is the need to *evaluate a large number of alternative actions*. Another characteristic of decision making problems is their *complexity*. The environment within which the decisions are to be made or the process about which one is trying to decide may be extremely complex; a conceptual model may afford the means of capturing the essence of such a situation. If our point of view or model is too restrictive, however, the original decision making process may be completely or partially misrepresented. On the other hand, if a conceptual model is to be workable, it must not be of such complexity that we cannot deal with its computational or data requirements.

Thus we can state some - perhaps conflicting - goals of a model:

1. *The model should reflect reality*: Realizing the real decision making framework is extremely complex and not exactly representable in conceptual terms; our model must nevertheless reflect to the extent possible the real world. There are always some trade-offs to be made with this goal. In general, as the model approaches reality its complexity becomes too great for out next goal. Thus the model builder is often faced with trying to capture the essence of the model within reasonable limits.
2. *The model must be solvable in terms of existing solution and/or analysis techniques*: It does not do us any good to construct a representation so complex as to defy analysis and solution. As will be discussed later in this chapter and later in the text, the idea of solvability can mean different things. In some cases, it is interpreted as the ability to change certain inputs to the model and to be able to observe the effect of such changes on the outputs of the model. In other cases, one may want to find the optimal set of inputs.
3. *The data needs of the model must be realistic*: The model must present realistic data requirements and not require either impossible amounts of data requirements and not require

either impossible amounts of data or uncollectable data. In one recently reported incident, the cost of data collection for a model of Canadian economy would itself have had an appreciable effect on the gross national product of the country. At any rate, this is a consideration that is often overlooked when constructing a model. To a large extent, a model is only as good as the data used to construct it, and if the necessary data cannot be generated the model cannot be put to use.

Thus, models represent abstractions or distillations of real-world decision making processes that we can get our hands on. Yet they represent all or most of the essential parts of the real-world process.

The importance of quantitative techniques

As can be seen from the references at the end of each chapter, each of the models covered here represents a mini-discipline of its own. In view of the body of knowledge surrounding each techniques, it is clear that one is not going to become an expert in any of the fields as a result of this course.

The study of these methods, however, does have some important benefits. By learning the fundamental principles of these various methods we can:

1. Better understand the limitations of each of the methods, so that they are not misused. For example - What are the implications of

treating a model with integer-valued variables by ordinary linear programming?

2. Better understand and interpret the solution to the model. For example - In a waiting-line model what is the trade-off between increased service and the cost to the system of providing such service?

3. Develop a basis for diagnosing the trouble if a technique yields no solution or a suspicious solution. for example - Is the transition matrix in a Markov process really stationery?

4. Better understand how to adapt existing models and applications to similar settings.

While all of the above benefits are important, they can be obtained only by acquiring an understanding of the underlying principles of the methods. This is particularly true with (4). As will be seen, the development of models and applications in a new setting can be extremely complex and time consuming. It is often to one's advantage to make use of any developments that have arisen in solving problems of a similar nature. Of course, for such transfers to be successful, an understanding of the effect of the assumptions is mandatory.

Finally, the advent of the new generation of computers is greatly facilitating the use of quantitative methods. The mini and micro computers provide tremendous computational capability that is certain to increase as the technology moves forward. Also the increased speed of problems that a few year ago were unsolvable. In order to increase the effectiveness of decision making processes, one needs to call upon this increased and increasing capability.

Successful applications

The purpose of this chapter is to motivate and excite the student about the potential for Operations Research/Management Science/ Decision Science in the real-world decision making environment. One of the best motivators is a brief look at some successful applications of Operations Research to problems in business and the public sector. As will be seen in this section and in subsequent chapters, the original applications of Operations Research lay within the military and private business. Recent applications, however, have included public areas such as state and local government, health care, and conservation of resources. These new areas, along with some new applications in business, foreshadow some exciting future possibilities for Operations Research.

It is not practical for us to give complete details of the applications that follow. These examples are for expository purposes only and are not meant to be complete. Additional details are found in the references. Additional sources of applications are the journals *Operations Research, Management Science, Interfaces, Operational Research Quarterly, Omega, Decision Science, Computers and Operations Research*, and others. The reader is urged to scan these publications for applications of interest.

Linear programming analysis of strip-mines land

A recent paper describes the application of linear programming to an area of current importance - the reclamation of strip-mined land. In many regions, state, local, or federal funds are available for rehabilitation of land currently being strip-mined, but large areas of previously strip-mined land lie unreclaimed for lack of funds. The purpose of the application described in the reference was to demonstrate to local and state agencies and local residents-by providing initial funding, fostering favorable legislation, and arousing interest- the economic benefits of reclaiming strip-mined land.

A linear programming model was constructed to evaluate several alternative uses of the land and to answer "What if ..." questions. The model indicated that cattle grazing would be the most productive use of the land. The model was then used to demonstrate the value of investment in the reclamation project.

As a result of this study the author was able to demonstrate that it would be economically feasible to reclaim 50,000 acres of strip-mined land in southeastern Kansan by utilizing the land for cattle grazing. The author constructed a linear programming model and an interactive computer program for evaluating the effect of reclaiming the land. Furthermore the author was able to persuade several landowners and the state government to share the cost of several demonstration projects to verify the results of the analysis. As a result of these demonstration projects a total of 5,000 acres has been reclaimed; the result has been an annual contribution of $1 million to the economy of the area.

Multiple criteria in decision making

One of the major assumptions of many models is that there is a single objective. This narrow choice of objective has caused difficulties in applications within large, complex organizations. Recent developments, termed goal programming or multi-criteria optimization, have allowed for the inclusion of several, perhaps conflicting or incommensurable objectives. An illustrative application has to do with the allocation of resources in an academic department within a major university.

The authors developed an interactive method for evaluating the trade-offs involved in allocating resources within the Graduate School of Management at UCLA. The faculty effort to be allocated must cover the three major activities of an academic department - teaching, service, and research. The *criteria* that were used to evaluate the allocation were: (1) number of graduate courses; (2) number of upper-division undergraduate courses; (3) number of lower-level undergraduate courses; (4) amount of effort devoted to service duties; and (5) amount of effort devoted to other activities including research, counseling, and so on. Given a fixed amount of resources, one can see that the above criteria are conflicting: one can be met only at the expense of another. Therefore, some trade-offs had to be evaluated.

As a result of the implementation of this model at the Graduate School of Management at UCLA, a shift in the allocation of resources was made away from teaching toward departmental duties. This shift reflected the need for such effort to start up a new graduate program. Also, the model has been to study the effects of proposed course changes and program changes. In each case one is able to assess the trade-offs among criteria.

Integer programming and forest management

A management problem of recurring interest deals with the management of forest resources including the construction of access roads. In order to manage forest it is necessary to have access to stands of trees and to be able to transport the cut trees to processing centers. In addition, scientific forest management dictates planning over several growing cycles or "rotations"; thus the time frame, in general, encompasses decades. This research applies integer programming to the management decisions concerned with forest management and access road building.

The general problem can be suggested by Figure The area of Figure has been divided into various timber stands. These stands may represent different ages or species that will be harvested at the same time. The objective of the model is to minimize hauling cost and road costs by choosing the best locations for the processing centers and the access roads. Also, since the time horizon may involve 60 to 200 years, one needs to take into account discounted net revenues for approximately 30 to 40 years.

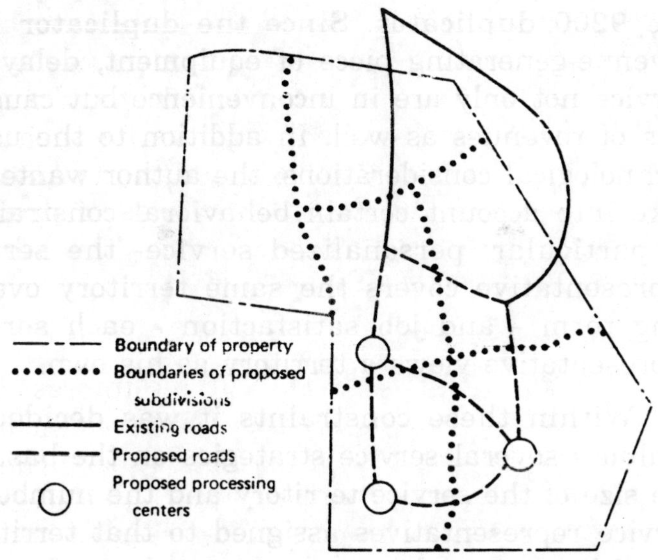

Figure

The authors, using data from the western slope of the Sierra Nevada in California, carried out their analysis on several 10-year management plans. The trials resulted in 6 percent savings in road costs and 1 percent increase in revenue from timber management. The model also provides a tool for analysing the effect of various strategies of road construction and timber management.

Waiting-line analysis of service time responses

One of the major applications of waiting-line or queuing models deals with the analysis of systems in which customers call for service and then await the arrival of the service representative to repair a nonfunctioning piece of equipment. The author applied such analysis to the service strategies of

Xerox Corporation for a new item of equipment-the 9200 duplicator. Since the duplicator is a revenue-generating piece of equipment, delays in service not only are in inconvenience but cause a loss of revenues as well. In addition to the usual technological considerations, the author wanted to take into account certain behavioral constraints, in particular: personalized service- the service representative covers the same territory over a long term - and job satisfaction - each service representative views a territory as his own.

Within these constraints it was decided to evaluate several service strategies on the basis of the size of the service territory and the number of service representatives assigned to that territory. A waiting-line model was constructed to reflect the service areas. As a result of the waiting-line analysis, based on response time, waiting-line length, and productivity, it was decided to deploy three-person teams. The analysis enabled Xerox to inform customers of the response time when they called for service and resulted in a 46 percent saving in total service costs.

Simulation of scheduling of surgical patients

One exciting application of OR/MS techniques involves health care and its delivery. In this paper, the authors discuss the use of GPSS as a means of evaluating the scheduling of surgical patients. Because it is impractical to try out scheduling ideas on real patients, the simulation model was used to gain valuable insights into various strategies.

The subject of the study was the operating and recovery facilities of a hospital St.Louis. Within the hospital there are five surgical suites and 12 recovery facilities that must be allocated to major and minor surgeries each day. Since the major surgeries tend to require extensive periods of time in both the operating room and recovery facilities, it is necessary to schedule uses of the facilities carefully. The purpose of the authors was to examine several strategies for scheduling patients into surgery consistent with the hospital's administrative guidelines. Strategies such as scheduling uses in the order they are requested; giving major surgeries priority over minor, serving those requiring longest surgery first, and so on, were evaluated using the simulation model. The hospital guidelines dictated that any strategy must be simple to avoid confusion and jockeying of patients at the last minute.

In the course of the simulation trials, the authors evaluated the various possible scheduling rules. The hospital administration was then able to compare the current scheduling policy with the alternative policies. In addition, as the demand on the surgical facilities increases the administration has a tool that can be used to alleviate some of the pressures. The results of analyzing the simulation model did present a short-run solution to the problem of scheduling a certain class of surgical patients.

Manpower management and markov chains

Operations research techniques have been

effectively applied to the management of manpower. In particular, such techniques have been used to study hiring and training requirements, the advancement of personnel through the organization, and turnover as a function of various organizational factors. In this example, the authors examined a technical department within a large corporation that exhibited a high turnover rate and faced a competitive job market.

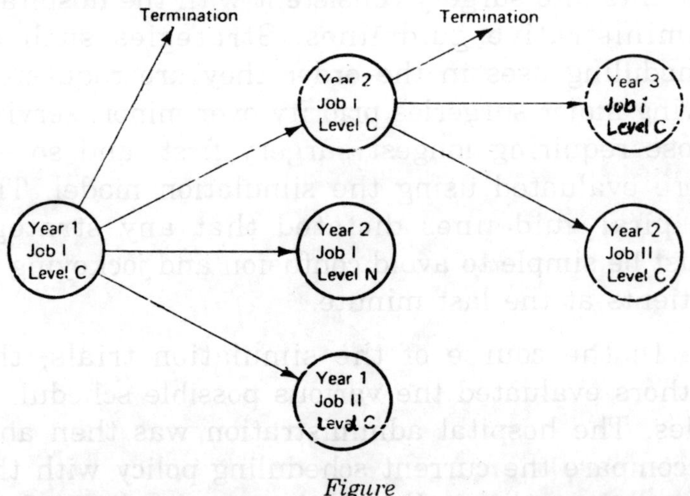

Figure

The purpose of the study was to model the hiring and promotion processes and provide a flow of relevant information for decision making regarding manpower management policies. As a result of their studies, the authors identified three job categories (I,II,III), two levels of employee competence (C,N), and a four-year time frame (1, 2, 3, 4) for movement among positions. A model of transitions among these states, including a termination state, was developed and tested against past company data. The transition diagram in part is given in Figure 1-2. The diagram depicts movement within grade with no promotion (1, I, C) to (2, I, C), movements with promotion (1, I, C) to (1, II, C), and so on, including termination initiated by either the company or the employee.

As a result of these studies, it was possible to evaluate the turnover rate in terms of the job market and the effect on the company. In addition, it was possible to test several management strategies against past data to observe the effect on the turnover rate as well as evaluate the effect on the company. That is, it is possible to assess the effect of changes in the promotion rates among job types, and to evaluate the effect of hiring at different levels.

Other cases presented in Part II show in detail the application of Operations Research/ Management Sciences/Decision Science to such diverse topics as fire station location, a CPA firm, police patrol-car scheduling, ammonia plant and its pollution, a state unemployment agency, and a chemical product/process decision.

Optimization, suboptimization, and simulation

As the examples of the previous section indicated, there are two methods of obtaining "solutions" to the model. The solution of models based on certain analytical results that can be used to characterize solutions in general are referred to as *optimization methods*. These methods, given a set of input data, generate the *optimal* solution to the particular model. There are many well known optimization methods-the simplex method of linear programming, the general results of waiting-line models, and so on. Within these methods there are those that guarantee the optimal solution for any such model-linear programming-and some that provide optimal solutions for restrictive classes-some integer program and waiting-line models-but for the general model no optimal characterization can be give. For this latter class of models, we must rely on the computational power of modern computers to provide evaluation via *simulation methods*. In general, as the complexity of a model increases, we must rely more heavily on simulation methods of obtaining numerical results. Simulation methods essentially perform experiments on the model by changing various parameters or variables and observing how the model responds to these changes. While the results are, in general, descriptive and not optimal, they do provide a means of analyzing very complex situations.

Another distinction to be drawn with regard to optimization is the area known as *suboptimization*. Suboptimization will mean two things in certain cases, it will mean the optimization of a portion of a larger system, or the optimization of a subsystem.

The first definition of suboptimization-a feasible but less than optimal solution-often applies to integer and multiple criteria programming. In these problems and some of their variants, the determination of *the optimal* solution can be extremely costly; instead, a good feasible solution will often suffice. While such a solution is not optimal, it may often provide valuable insights and/or savings when applied to the process being modeled.

The second definition of suboptimization-the optimization of subsystem-is appropriate whenever we are dealing with large complex organizations. Typically in such situations, one cannot deal with the entire organization. Thus, while we may be optimizing the operation of one department, that optimum may be suboptimal with regard to the overall operation. Since the obvious resolution of this problem-modeling the entire organization-may not be feasible, one must be content with models of various subsystems. This question is difficult to resolve in general and awaits further research. One can argue that if the model and its results provide a better operating scheme within a subsystem, even though the scheme may be suboptimal with regard to the larger system, the entire system benefits.

Implementation and limitations of or

Section 4 of this chapter attempted to illustrate some of the successful implementations of Operations Research/Management Science techniques. These point to some past and future applications and areas of interest. In the literature of the area there has been some concern about the implementation of these techniques.

Two professional societies, The Operations Research Society of America (*Orsa*) and The

Institute of Management Sciences (TIMS) have devoted a publication, *Interfaces,* to highlighting successful implementations of the techniques of Operations Research/Management Science. In addition, each year a group within The Institute of Management Sciences sponsors a competition for the best implementation of Operations Research/ Management Science in either the public or private sector. As a result of these efforts more and more successful implementations are being brought to the attention of the profession.

It has been said that the theory of Operations Research/Management Science has greatly outdistanced its implementation, and that the discipline is only now beginning to catch up. There have been a number of reasons for the lack of publication and acceptance of the results of Operations Research/Management Sciences among the most important are:

1. Successful implementations within a company are often maintained as confidential to avoid giving any information to competitors. As a result many publications contain only the theoretical development and give no hint as to the potential applicability. Even if there are no major problems of proprietary information in successful private-sector applications of management science, there is a real cost involved in disseminating information. This cost arises from the time and effort required to prepare the results of a project in a form suitable for journal publication, and from the

expense involved in disseminating results at professional meetings. For the most part, there have been no incentives for private practitioners to public their results.

2. Firms are resistant to change. A firm has a policy or strategy that has worked in the past; so why change now? This is particularly common attitude when the results have derogatory implications with regard to organizational policies.

3. The model and/or its results are based on highly mathematical analyses that are not clearly explained to the user of the results. Conversely, the model may be a gross oversimplification of the real process, and the results of the model are useless with regard to the actual decision making process.

4. Additional reasons that have been pointed out include:

The problem "solved" is not the problem facing the organization.

The solution is reached after a decision has been made.

The resources expended in reaching the solution are greater than the savings achieved from implementing the solution.

The data used in the solution are wrong.

The model builder and the manager have different goals.

These statements are true for obvious reasons.

From the standpoint of the practitioner of operations research or management science or the decision sciences, what steps can be taken to assist in solving the right problem with a methodology that is correct, trusted, and understood? In other words, how can the profession enhance the chances that the results of a study will be implemented?

The foremost principle of successful operations research is the *involvement of the management of the organization*. This involvement is important for all the reasons mentioned above. Further, it keeps the project focused on real problems facing the organization. Since it is the management of the organisation that is responsible for addressing these problems, their involvement keeps a decision science effort focused on the right problem. Still further, this involvement helps bring understanding of the methodology to the managers. Their involvement serves to a large extent as a educational exchange for those managers who may not be familiar with decision science techniques and those analysts who are not familiar with the problem. Finally, the manager of an organization often has much more interest in pursuing the implementation of an analysis that represents a substantial investment of management's time and efforts. Perhaps this principle of management involvement explains what some see as a trend in which practitioners of the decision sciences function in small groups, each focusing on a part of an organisation and its immediate management, rather than a large group serving as a consultant to all parts of the organization.

The aim of this book is to bridge the gap between technique and implementation. Our basic premise is that in order to succeed in, or to understand, the implementation of a technique one must first understand the basic ideas of the technique itself. On the other hand, we do not want to ignore the setting in which the technique is to be applied. As you proceed through the book you will notice many references to applications of the topics of each chapter. These references offer valuable amplification of the text material being covered.

In an attempt to draw together the quantitative techniques of the text and actual decision making processes, the second part of the book presents several detailed cases.

The reference already made to the manger's task, and to the duties arising from it, suggest that the management burden is a complex one. That this is true in practice can be seen from the mental and physical strain to which executives are subject, as denoted by the incidence of ailments that have come to be recognised as typical of the executive, ulcers of the stomach and duodenum and coronary thrombosis. The increasing attention being paid to the health of the executives had led to his being given some relief through relaxation aimed to alleviate the anxiety of his task. Enlightened companies have even introduced the "sabbatical" year of leave of absence from company affairs to permit their top executives to enjoy a complete change of outlook away from the day-to-day cares of the major management position. It is not possible to permit every manager to benefit from such a concession, nor is there the same need for relaxation at every level of management. This is not to say that the task is progressively lightened so that the duties are correspondingly less onerous at lower levels of management, but the consequences of error are generally less serious

The manager can cope with the task allotted to him only when he possesses the skills necessary for the satisfactory accomplishment of the resulting duties. These skills are to be compared with those needed for hand working, i.e. the traditional skills of the craftsman. Skills in this context are developed as a result of practice so that dexterity is achieved in the exercise of the acts associated with working. The result is a developed talent that is separate and distinct from any common accomplishment that everyone has achieved. The development of the skills is a lengthy process. It is usually a development period spent under introduction as a novice or learner, so that an apprenticeship is served in order to become a skilled practitioner The term "mysteries" is used in some trades to indicate the characteristics of certain features of the skills that are passed on during the training process, but not readily known or understood by the ordinary man.

It is not possible to state the skills of

management as simply as those of the craftsman, nor are they acquired so readily. Nevertheless a parallel can be drawn between the two types of activity. The manager must be capable of selecting the correct method of working, and for this he needs skill in the use of the alternatives in order that he can recognise the features of their employment. There are certain "tools" that the manager uses and in the use of which he must have a measure of skill as well as an aptitude for the acquisition of the necessary skills. This demands specific innate traits of personality, since the principal skills of the management act are associated with the guidance and supervision of people. Unlike the craftsman, however, the manager need not possess a high degree of dexterity since his duties involve the thought processes rather than the use of hand and eye as in the physical manipulation of materials.

The variety of skills exercised in carrying out the management task arises largely from the broad range of duties devolving upon the manager. Human skills are needed for the direction of people, and these are of prime importance to the manager since he is fundamentally concerned with getting things done by others rather than with himself doing work like the manipulation of materials by the use of machines or muscles. Arising from the duty to make arrangements that contribute to the achievement of the defined objectives, the manager will be concerned with the economy of utilisation of material resources. Many of the "tools" of management permit him to exercise skill in the specification of the arrangements for the discharge of his task effectively. An additional instance of the variety of skills is to be found in the manager's duties in connection with the selection of techniques and the methods to be used for accomplishing specified objectives. This demands the employment of a highly developed skill for making decisions that turn out to be right more often than wrong.

Human skills

Management is recognised principally by the inseparable element of concern for people that is always of great consequence. Skills are therefore needed relative to this human element so that:

the way in which people are treated;

the manner of giving orders and instructions;

the direction of human activities generally,

contribute to the effectiveness of management. It is necessary, therefore, to consider in some detail the various individual skills that go to make up the manager's ability for dealing with the human element.

Without implying that it is the most important, the first skill to be mentioned in connection with the human element is in the correct use of power. Every manager is able to command obedience from the people for whom he is responsible, as authority comes with position. It is possible therefore for any manager, if he so desires, to make use of this authority to insist upon certain activities being carried out by his subordinates even though these are not strictly demanded by the circumstances of the work. Power can be wielded in a spiteful way if the person with authority wants to exploit his position. It is also possible to insist upon the strict interpretation of rules and regulations so that every workman has to comply rigidly with the letter rather than with the spirit of the written word. The skilled manager does none of these things. He recognises that his power comes from the group whose activities he is supervising. It is not something separate and distinct that he can treat as a stick with which to beat the members of his working group. The correct use of power involves the employment of authoritarian command only for the purposes demanded by the situation, and in the light of the defined objectives. Power is not to be used as a means of gratifying the whims of the manager. The skilled exponent of the management arts recognises this and acts accordingly.

Associated with the use of power is the skill of co-ordination. The activities of groups of people can be harmonised most readily when authority is employed correctly. There will then be a resultant desire to co-operate so that the unification of activity is made more effective. Although procedures are available for ensuring co-ordination the fundamental requirement is for the manager to be so skilled in the handling of human affairs that he is assured of co-operation by the spontaneous action of those within the group. Co-ordination does not then need to be imposed by the use of any specialist techniques. The skill of promoting co-ordination arises from the assessment of each person so that it is possible to judge his foibles, strength and weakness. The treatment meted out to each individual subordinate can then be appropriate to him as a person, with the full harmonising of effort as a result.

A most important skill in the "handling" of people is the ability to criticise without doing lasting harm. The respect accorded by one person to another is based on many factors, but it can so easily be destroyed if the atmosphere between them becomes strained. When a subordinate considers that he has been criticised more harshly than circumstances demand, or has been reprimanded in the wrong way, especially if it has been done in the hearing of other people, there will be a loss of respect with the consequent lowering of the manager's authority of personality. The skill of criticism lies in correctly allocating blame to the extent appropriate to the circumstances, but to do this in a manner productive of future effort rather than destructive by discouragement of the worker reprimanded. If a person is over-criticised, or is reprimanded unnecessarily, the result can easily be lasting in its effect by sowing the seeds of antagonism between the manager and the person subject to his authority.

The need for criticism will not be present when everyone is doing his job properly and to the best of his ability. A consequent skill needed by the manager is in connection with training so that there will be no barrier to the success of his subordinates in carrying out the work expected of them. It is an obligation of the manager to train his subordinates and so contribute to overall effectiveness by the best use of existing resources. An associated skill is the ability to assess the present ability of people in relation to the work assigned to them, so that the need for additional practice or broadening of experience can be determined. There is also the need for the manager to train his own deputy so that no break in continuity occurs when he is temporarily absent, or leaves through retirement or promotion. By permitting the deputy to understudy him so that he becomes familiar with the character of a different job of work at a higher level, and by developing the deputy's talent so that he achieves confidence and self-reliance, there will accrue a promotional potentiality for the benefit of the undertaking.

When subordinates are self-confident and capable of carrying out extended tasks, it becomes possible to delegate more and more wok to them according to the everchanging needs of a thriving and expanding company. The skills of delegation are to be found, initially, in the choice of the delegate to act on the manager's behalf with all the requisite aplomb. It will be reliable that this skill is associated with the skills involved in delegation is that of withdrawal on the part of the manager. There has to be an act of watching by keeping in touch, but this must be done in such a way that there is no suggestion of lack of confidence in the delegate's ability. The skills of delegation are the most difficult to develop in the manager, especially if at an earlier stage in his career, he has been accustomed to doing things for himself.

From this detailing of the skills necessary for directing people, it will be evident that there is no simple or single talent required by the manager. In the use of power, in encouragement and co-ordination, in the manner of his criticism, and also by training and by delegation, skills are used in the carrying out of the duties imposed by regard for the human element of the manager's task.

Technical skills

The second group of skills to which reference was made earlier, is that concerned with the economy of utilisation of material resources. Some technical skills arise from knowledge and experience of the work being done. They are not so general in character as those attaching to the human aspect, but it is in connection with this technical aspect of the manager's job that the greatest aid is available from specialists. Although it is not possible to segregate regard for people from the work of the manager, it is possible to provide specialist assistance in regard to the many facets of the technicality of his work. His own skills then lie in the interpretation of the advice given to him so as to arrive at the correct association of the various ideas presented to him. Some of these ideas will be in conflict, either with each other or with the sense of the manager, and their resolution will result in a decision being taken on such practices and procedures as lie within the manager's authority.

Decision making

The decision-making act has already been shown to be an important part of the manager's duties. It is now seen to be related to the technological nature of his work, but it is also a feature of the human aspect. In both respects the skills of decision making are important. One of these skills relates to the manger's ability to foresee future occurrences and to plan accordingly. This brings an imaginative concept into decision making which removes the manager from the realm of directing operations purely by experience. He must be capable of prediction. Then, the knowledge of the job he has accumulated over the years can be employed to plan the activity to suit the predicted occurrence or circumstance. In his decision making the manager must constantly think of the future. The trends that can be envisaged help him to bring to bear the decisiveness that is fruitful of effective long-term guidance. He will then avoid acting merely expediently and so creating a need for additional decisions at frequent intervals, and consequently a lack of continuity of undirectional activity.

Information and intuition

Too great a reliance on business "flair" is a negative skill in decision making. There is a tendency among practical managers to exercise intuition in arriving at decisions and to base their conclusions only on this. For consistent accuracy of guidance, there must be a basis of fact rather than one of uninformed opinion. This implies the need for a skill in interpreting fact so that the right conclusion is drawn from it. Information should be the basis of opinion. Information combined with opinion forms a basis for a sound conclusion. A decision is taken when the conclusion is reached. As information is so vital, it is obviously desirable for the manager to keep himself informed of all the facts that influence his job directly and indirectly. For example, he must keep up to date on matters of staffing, on Trade Union activities, on world economic trends, especially when new international events affecting trade are likely to arise. In the field of politics there may be some trend that is of importance to him because it bears upon decisions of consequence for the future conduct of his business. The researches of science or technology may disclose improvements on which the eventual prosperity of a firm will depend. Sources of information are boundless, yet the busy manager needs to devote sufficient time to the task of keeping up to date with all items of information that may affect his decisions. Such keeping in touch with the changing world around him is a skill that must be practiced by the manager if his decisions are to be appropriate and reliable.

Although business flair is not itself sufficient for a decision, it is never entirely absent when a manager had to decide. To the skill of judgement on which the accuracy of a decision depends, there must be added the skill of timing the application of the decision. Both these demand an intuitive "flair" or "feel" for a situation. Hunch is not a bad thing if it is a highly developed skill, but it can be thoroughly unreliable when adopted nonchalantly as the basis for decisions.

It is not sufficient merely for a decision to be made, even when all the available information has been taken into account during its formulation. The decision must be applied if activity is to flow from it, but the timing of the application may critically affect the adequacy of the activity. For this reason, the art of knowing when to take action is a further important skill of the manager.

Communications

Having made his decision on timing, the manager must communicate the decision to those whose actions will be needed to put it into effect. A requisite for this is skill in the use of language to establish understanding. A high proportion of communications is passed by word of mouth, so the skill of speaking is important in this respect and it may even need to be the developed art of public speaking, rather than merely that of face-to-face talking. Such a need for a more advanced form of oral expression is common in large firms and in positions of top management, but it is not a vital requirement for the majority of managers. In addition to facility of oral expression the manager must have sufficient clerical ability to enable him to express his ideas effectively in writing. For permanence of record, or for bridging geographical distance, the written communication is an indispensable feature of modern business life. The manager must therefore be skilled in that form of expression. Whatever the means of communication used, it is not solely the order of instruction arising from the decision that has to be communicated. There is also the need for explanations of the nature of the changes that are taking place and the reasons for them. The requisite skill in this connection is the ability to disseminate ideas clearly and succinctly so that the crux of a matter is quickly conveyed and readily understood.

Management personality

Such a formidable array of skills suggests a veritable superman as the characteristic management personality. The manager does not, however, need to possess a highly developed talent in all these skills simultaneously, as the needs of each job vary. The qualifications need by the manager depend upon the type of management task assigned to him. In the higher stratum of management the duties of the manager are concerned principally with the direction of people and the skills associated with the art of management. There is such a degree of remoteness from the technical operations of the undertaking, with an accompanying buffer of supervisors interposed between them and the manager, that job knowledge is not a significant qualification. It may seem a peculiarity of industry and commerce that a man can become a chief executive of a large and substantial business enterprise without any technological preparation or qualification. Such a situation emphasises the need at top management level for personality rather than technical job knowledge. It is the opinion of many people that the man who has been trained principally as a scientist or technologist is often unsuited for a position that involves the direction of others. He tends to be immersed in his technology to the extent of being myopic about other aspects of management. It is an outstanding feature of present trends that many top management positions are filled by men with a broad arts background, in preference to those more experienced in the technicalities of the work to be directed. There is no longer the need to proceed upwards through an undertaking by promotion or succession in order to achieve a top level position. It has become increasingly apparent that the chief executive can be very successful even when he has had no former connection with the type of product or service provided by the undertaking.

Because of the change in duties and the consequent alteration in emphasis on the constituent duties involved in carrying out the management task in different types of company, and at the various levels at which management activity has to be undertaken, it is possible only to generalise in idealist terms about the desirable management personality, and to suggest the characteristics and personality traits that can be regarded as desirable in anyone made responsible for the activities of group of people. The preliminary requirement of any director of activity is *vitality*. A lethargic approach does not inspire confidence, nor does the person who is handicapped by poor physical health. The manager must be healthy and possess sufficient vitality to set the tone for the activity of those for whom he is responsible. The character of the manager should be above reproach so that it inspires confidence in his honesty of purpose. There must be a strong sense of justice in his manner of handling matters referred to him, accompanied by a keen interest in the personal problems of subordinates. Ideally, the manager should also have sustained moral courage to enable him to stand out for the right and proper action required by situations as he interprets them.

In temperament he should be a sanguine person inclined to look on the bright side of affairs. He should have an equable temperament with an ability to control the expression of his feelings. It is undesirable for the manager to have a tendency to panic, or to lose his sense of balanced judgement under the pressure of events. He should be a dynamic extrovert person, remote from the coldness and aloofness that is sometimes such a barrier to the scientist in a management post. provision of persons to assist him with his complex task. This is an extension of the personality of the manager by the use of aides, without restricting his function or responsibility in any way. The real significance of this procedure is that the manager's attention can be focused on the main aspects of his task, since he can rely upon his aides to perform the detailed work and relevant routine. The main purpose of the use of staff assistance in this way is to facilitate the recruitment and training of managers without the need to employ only the super-talented.

Aides can be used for many purposes. Failure to appreciate this fact can lead to confusion when consideration is being given to the application of the underlying "staff" principle. If the manager being so assisted is a general manager, however competent, he is likely to require some specialist staff assistance in areas of knowledge in which he is not himself well qualified. Accountancy, for example, is a specialist function the technicalities of which are often unfamiliar to the works manager. In such a case, a financial or costing aide would provide valuable staff assistance. On the other hand, the manager may have arrived at his position after gaining his experience outside the broad field of endeavour he now has to command. In such a situation the services of a general staff assistant may be invaluable with the activities of command and co-ordination that are inseparable from the management position, but in which the appointed manager is not skilled or experienced. The third type of staff assistance is of a personal type, and may really be provided by a confidential secretary, but with a prestige title like

"Personal Assistant" or "P.A". This enables the manager to avoid certain irritating details of his office and results in the presentation to him of an orderly routine of activity, with arrangements for meetings, interviews, and so on, determined for him. The documents, reports and statistics he need to peruse are also made available in such a way that he has to spend the minimum time in assimilating their contents and drawing significant conclusions from them.

The second method of affording relief to the manager is therefore by the appointment of aides so that any limitations of the manager's qualities or qualifications are not reflected in his work. The "staff" officers so established may be for general, special or personal activities, but the common feature of them all is that they do not have any command responsibility. They are merely extensions of their manager's personality with no authority in their own right.

Management style

An observer of management in action will find some very different approaches; two people can be seen to achieve the same objective by very dissimilar methods. Is it possible to make a valid comparative assessment of the way in which each manages? An interesting effort to do so has been based on a concept of management style.

We are nearly all acquainted with the distinction between authoritarian and democratic leadership but more recently there has been introduced the *managerial grid*, the creation of

Dr. Robert R.Blacke, one-time of the Department of Psychology in the University of Texas and subsequently a training consultant.

The grid is an attempt to evaluate management style on the assumption that a manager has two general areas of concern, namely (a) people and (b) production, a proportion of his time and energy being devoted to each.

Blake's Grid provides a 1-9 scale so that a manager can be given a rating for each area, nine being the highest rating in either case. To quote a few possible ratings:

1, 1 is impoverished management, with ineffective performance in production and lazy and indifferent workpeople.

1, 9 is "country club management" - production is incidental to lack of conflict and the preservation of good fellowship.

5, 5 is middle of the road management, with some drive generated for output but with nobody exerting themselves to their full capacity.

9, 1 with a high rating for concern with output and a very low rating for concern for people; this is sometimes known as task management, men and women in the work situation being looked on as a commodity much as machines and materials are. In such an environment, to challenge orders and procedures in interpreted as a lack of co-operation. Little attention is paid to thoughts, attitudes and feelings.

9, 9 is a team management, with high productivity flowing from the integration of task and human requirements.

This is a simple, even over-simplified, concept and a manager who has mastered the elements of the "management style" concept should b able to give a general assessment of performance. He cannot be truly quantitative in his appraisals and the approach is very generalised; yet it has been found helpful by serving managers.

Blake's managerial grid has not been the only approach to this problem of appraising management style. An alternative, Reddin's 3 Dimensional Grid, distinguishes eight types of manager. They range from the "deserter" who is ineffective and avoids responsibility to the ideal executive. Reddin has evolved a self-administered Management Style Diagnosis Test so that managers may recognise their own style and alter it if this is found advisable.

3 Management Education: Programmes and Systems

In establishing and operating organizations, management it an essential elements in performing work efficiently and effectively. The organization, being a social and technical system of consciously co-ordinated activities of two or more persons, could not continue to reach objectives for any sustained period of time without management. Likewise, the ability to successfully meet the challenges of complex changes requires outstanding managerial expertise and leadership such that both the organization and society will benefit.

Goals are reached through the utilization of many resources, such as personnel, machines, money and technology. These resources, however, are incomplete without the presence and operation of management. As a central activity in the life of all organizations, management is omnipresent in out society, although it is rather nebulous in form and structure and not always apparent to the causal observer. One of the early scholars and writers in the field of management - Henri Fayol - stated that the nervous system in the animal sphere bears close comparison with the managerial activities of a social organization. For our purposes, the implication of this statement is that management is essential in achieving a coordination of activities when people band together for a common purpose.

Management viewed as a process

Various definitions of management exist, many of which highlight the nature and importance of management. Based upon the viewpoint of this book, *management is defined as the process of planning, organizing, actuating, and controlling an organization's operations in order to achieve a coordination of the human and material resources essential in the effective and efficient attainment of objectives.* The elements or activities in this process are referred to as *management functions* and must be performed by all persons in managerial positions, whether administrators, directors, generals, department heads, or first line supervisors. Before discussing the management functions, it should be clearly understood that the management process is best described by the functions or activities performed rather than by the status or rank held by certain individuals in an organization. In fact, management is neither the privilege nor the responsibility of only the top members of an organizations, but the work of all people whose tasks are involved with reaching goals and achieving objectives through a coordination of effort.

Relevance of the management functions

In guiding and directing an organization, certain inputs are required before a system can create desired outputs. Illustrates that the management process of planning, organizing, actuating, and controlling provides the coordinative effort that assists in producing desirable outputs in the form of various goods and services. The potential impact or importance of the functions depends upon the authority possessed by the manager performing the functions, the stage of development of the organization, and various environmental factors, including government regulations, competitors, and consumer demand. In creating a new organization, the performance of these functions would normally follow the order of planning, organizing, actuating, and controlling. For an established organisation, a manager at one particular time may be performing any one or a combination of these functions. Although definitions vary, the management functions can be characterized as:

1. *Plan* the objectives, strategies, policies, procedures, methods, standards, and programs required in directing the organization's human and material resources for future time spans. Plans establish the framework or boundaries in which people make decisions and carry out assigned activities. They are developed through the planning process and anticipate future events, problems, and relationships. In this sense, planning refers to (1) deciding what to do how to do it before action is taken, and (2) developing a

series of alternative plans to guide action toward desired goals. Thus, as a formal process, planning implies a rationalistic approach which recognizes problems, develops alternative courses of action, evaluates relevant information, assesses the possible consequences of each alternative, and selects a best course of action.

2. *Organize* required human and material resources so that relevance and coordination are provided to unite the various parts into a meaningful whole. Organizing involves a division of total wok into specialties; a grouping of similar activities; an identification of desired relationships between groups;; a delegation of authority; and a consideration of the social and economic consequences associated with various organizational designs. In general, then, organizing is concerned with combining people work to be done, and physical factors into a meaningful structure of authority that will contribute to an achievement of goals. The formal structure, however, is only part of the organisational framework. Various informal groups are also created by employees and the resulting interrelationships influence behavior patterns within an organization as much as formally established authority levels.

3. *Actuate* personnel to the degree that behaviour is consistent and congruent with that perceived as necessary for accomplishing organizational goals. In this sense, actuation includes motivation, leadership, communication, training, and personal influence. As such, this

function is often discussed as directing and executing the work that must be done. In addition, while proving direction for behavior, actuating becomes closely interrelated with the other functions of planning, organizing, and controlling.

4. *Control* by monitoring current operations and comparing results to goals and other standards of performance. If current activities and/or results deviate from original plans, corrective action is required to get things back on path. Such action might take the form of repairing faulty machinery or equipment, modifying human behavior, reorganizing a department, or changing the original plan and its corresponding standards.

Finally, when two or more individuals band together to achieve a common goal, *coordination* is required to blend the efforts of all members for an efficient and effective result. Thus, coordination is not considered as a basic management function, but is the result of interplay among the other functions. In addition, it is important to realize that an identification and understanding of the management functions has been a gradual and evolutionary process. One way to view the development of the functions, then, is to look back into history at some of their early applications. Through this method, students of management can observe the commonality of planning, organizing, actuating, and controlling that has existed in all great organizaitons. And, by recognizing common patterns, a framework for scientific investigation and research can be established for the development of more efficient organizations in out present-day society.

Historical applications of management

Applications of management concepts go back as far as early primitive tribes. Anthropologists relate that the concept of authority was very apparent in many early societies and that survival depended to a great extent upon an adherence to a hierarchy of authority. In later civilizations, management planning and organizing became more apparent, particularly in the building of the pyramids in ancient Egypt.

One of the earliest and most interesting applications of management is related in the Biblical story of Moses and exodus of the Israelites from Egypt. In the story, Jethro - Moses' father-in-law- advised him that he should choose able men as rulers over thousand hundreds, fifties, and tens since he (Moses) did not have the time and strength to personally judge all of the people. In this story, an important managerial concept is exemplified when Moses accepted the staff advice and counsel from Jethro. Also the organizing ability of Moses is shown through his delegation of authority to others in order to create a hierarchy of authority. The statement that every great matter should be brought to Moses, but every small matter should be judged by the people themselves, is an example controlling exceptional and significant activities. And, the personnel selection and training of "able men out of all Israel" illustrates the importance of the actuating function.

In early Greece management concepts were reorganized by Plato, particularly the importance of a specialization of labor as a means for increasing productivity. Socrates, who felt that management competence differs from technical competence, noted that a good manager in one organization could, in the right situation, be a good manager in another type of organization. Furthermore, descriptions of the ancient Greek city-states indicate that the institutional functions of government· were highly organised and managed.

Other good applications of management can be seen in the early Greek and Roman military organizations. From Alexander the Great to Caesar, the functions of planning, acquiring, organizing, actuating, and controlling were extremely important in winning battles and wars. In advance of a battle, for example, Caesar used intelligent and loyal commanders of his legions for assistance in planning, and then delegated authority to his commanders to provide a coordinated and effective fighting force.

The vast domains of Rome were held together by an elaborate set of roads and by a hierarchical structure of authority. Rulers of the empire's geographical territories, dioceses, and divisions were delegated appropriate authority to make decisions applicable to each unit. Thus, coordination achieved by planning, organizing, and the use of discipline explained to a great extent the Roman genius in ruling its vast domain. Not unlike the Roman Empire, the early

Roman Catholic Church was also faced with organizing the efforts of a large group of people spread over a wide geographical area. The organizational efforts of a the early church, however, were quite different from those used by the Romans. Through the Pope, the church retained a great deal of authority with a fairly large number of people reporting to superiors at each level. Particularly important in this respect was the use of staff personnel who advised the Pope.

Many of today's managerial concepts can also be found in an interesting historical description of the building of Venetian ships during the Renaissance period of the fifteenth and sixteenth centuries. The Arsenal of Venice, a government shipyard that produced military ships on a production line basis, embraced modern management practices of warehousing; assembly line; personnel management; standardization; and controlling of inventory, costs, and financial accounts.

The use of carpenters, oar makers, fasteners of timbers and planks, mast makers, caulkers, etc., emphasized the use and importance of a division of labor. The building of the galleys was divided into three stages: (1) framing by the carpenters, (2) fastening the plankings and then building the cabins and superstructures by carpenters and caulkers and (3) the final assembly.

All equipment and parts, such as rudders, gun

carriages, small parts, rigging, oars, and arms were manufactured in separate craft shops under the watchful eyes of supervisors who directed the technical work, provided needed materials and supplies, and inspected completed work. The production of these items was arranged along a canal so that a galley could be launched and then fitted with all of its equipment and arms in the final assembly state. For this purpose the galley was towed along the canal and the equipment and arms were placed on the craft through the windows of warehouses along the canal.

The Arsenal was highly efficient, productive, and fast in the production of ships that made Venice a mighty naval power. In turn, these achievements were brought about because the Lords of the Arsenal performed the management functions as a full-time activity and, at the same time, had technical experts and craftsmen to perform the work.

Beginning of contemporary management thought

Henri Fayol, a Frenchman who managed the Commentary-Four chambault mining company from 1888 to 1918, developed one of the earliest and most comprehensive theories of general management. In three years as managing director of the mining company, Fayol had move it from a declining firm to one of France's greatest combines by developing and applying various managerial concepts. Many of his writings are still quite applicable and have contributed greatly to contemporary management thinking. In recognition of his work, Fayol is considered the "father" of the management process point of view. Yet, his work was not translated from French into English until 1925 and received little attention in the United States until 1949. thus, applications of his work were delayed for more than twenty years, thereby slowing the advancement of management thought in the United States.

Since several of Fayol's ideas assist in clarifying the nature and content of modern-day management, they deserve added consideration. Three such concepts are: (1) management competence differs from technical competence; (2) the scientific nature of management; and (3) the university concept of management.

Management competence differs from technical competence

Fayol suggested that managerial practices should be distinguished from the technical competence found in engineering, production, marketing, and finance. All business operations, according to Fayol, can be divided into six independent operations.

1. Producing operations
2. Commercial operations
3. Financial operations
4. Security operations
5. Accounting operations
6. Managerial-Administrative operations

Without question, managers or administrators cannot completely divorce themselves from the performance of certain specialized types of work, such as production or selling. For example, a sale manager is often involved in actual selling activities. Likewise, the production supervisor in an assembly department may work closely with subordinates. However, a distinguishing characteristic between managers and other employees stems from the fact that managers plan, organize, actuate, and exercise control over the actual technical operations of an organization. Thus, managers must have a working knowledge of certain technical operations, but they are not normally responsible for performing such operations themselves.

To expand, we see that top management positions are generally associated with fewer technical responsibilities than middle or lower-level management jobs. This is especially true in large organizations where, as one moves into higher managerial positions, the decisional process is less likely to be structured around some specific technical skill. This means that managerial advancement requires an ability to balance various organizational activities such as engineering, marketing, and finance. In this sense, managerial competence requires a coordination of overall interests and operations in reaching organizational objectives. Of course, achieving a coordination of interests in organizations interfaced with a complex and dynamic environment may result in two or more top level executives sharing the work load. In any event, effective managerial problem solving requires that alternatives be considered and evaluated from a broad perspective. Narrow technical views will not suffice.

Scientific nature of management

To further the development of a general theory, Fayol suggested that management should be studied from a scientific approach. In this sense, scientific inquiry would follow the guidelines identified by Rene Descartes in his *Discourse on Method* and should be used to determine:

1. *What* exists in the real work, as derived from empirical evidence.
2. *Why* a given phenomenon behaves as it does.
3. *How* to classify data related to a real world phenomenon.

Through scientific inquiry, then, a systematic body of knowledge can be developed that helps to explain relationships between various situational factors. Thus, the goal of scientific inquiry is to provide an understanding of various events in nature so as to better predict their subsequent impact on future courses of action.

With some changes, the steps of the scientific method have been employed in managerial problem solving and are generally expressed as:

1. Define, delineate, and state the problem that is to be solved.
2. Review the literature on the problem area and

discuss it with informed sources and experts. All facts that have a bearing on the problem are thoroughly investigated.

3. Develop a statement of hypothesis or a tentative solution to the problem.
4. Collect primary and secondary data. Organize and classify all relevant information.
5. Analyze the data, as related to the problem and hypothesis, by interpreting existing causal relationships.
6. Set forth the findings, conclusions, and recommendations that depend upon the correlation between causal relationships.
7. Implement recommendations and monitor action to determine the success of the solution and the validity of the findings.

Although managers have not been able to follow these steps as completely as in the physical and life sciences, it should not be assumed that the scientific method cannot be applied to the practice of management. In fact, some management scholars feel that, since management tends towards being a science, "a scientific approach to management cannot wait until an exact science of management can be developed." To some degree, such scholars feel that principles and a body of management knowledge can be derived from experience and observation. In other words, management credence need not be totally based on the scientific method. Due to this belief, the use of the term *principle* also varies in management literature and does not necessarily imply a fact proven through extensive and controlled research. In fact, due to the human element in organizations, it is doubtful that there can ever be exact and precise control exercised over managerial experimentation and research.

Management principles

One way to classify portions of our current management knowledge is through the use of principles which may be regarded as general statements of organizational and management behavior. such principle are stated in a form that identifies cause and effect relationships. In other words, principles assist in predicting the result of a particular action. Thus, principles provide guides to thought and action. In doing so, they contribute to an avoidance of mistakes by providing insights into possible results. consequently, as related to management, the advocates of principles feel that their application will bring about good results; that is, a more effective and efficient achievement of organizational goals.

Many of the principles of management stated in the Appendix at the end of this chapter have, in fact, been utilized by practicing managers with great success. Yet, many successful operations can also be found where these principles have been violated. Furthermore, some scholars note that the environments of management may have become too complex for principles to be applied and used in the development of a general theory of management. In this sense, it is evident that given environmental conditions and managerial judgment have a great deal to do with whether management principles are applicable to real world situations.

To summarize, we know that a principle in the physical sciences is meaningful only when developed through the scientific method of conceptualizing, hypothesizing, and theorizing. Thus, arduous investigation is required to develop realistic and purposeful principles. For an inexact science such as management, however, the starting point may well be that of developing principles based on observation and experience. Then, through scientific investigation one can seek to prove or disprove them. Although such procedures lack the accurate predictability of those in the physical sciences, the avenues of experience, experiment, and discussion are still superior toe the utilization of a straight trail and error approach in the practice of management. Of course, it must be recognized that the resulting principles are guides and not absolutes. Nevertheless, they contribute to a better understanding of management and are important in all managerial decision making.

Management concepts

Regardless of the nature of management principles, the starting point for a truly scientific approach to the study of management may be found in the development and classification of concepts. Management concepts are no more than ideas developed by generalizing from reality. However, they must be stated clearly and concisely since ambiguity leads to misinterpretation and confusion. Once concepts have been identified they must then grouped according to some classification system if they are to permit a generalization of events having a common resemblance.

Although not necessarily described as such, a large number of concepts may be found in management literature. At the present time, however, there has been no concerted effort by management scholars to bring these concepts together under a meaningful classification system. Possibly the future will see their unification brought about through the systematic conceptualization provided by the systems approach.

Since history indicates that systems of management existed in ancient civilizations, it is indeed strange that the activities associated with goal achievement represent one of the last areas about which we have attempted to discover more useful and accurate knowledge. For example, major scientific discoveries were made in the life and physical sciences 100 to 400 years before Fayol's writings. But, it was not until about the time of Fayol and F.W. Taylor that management was considered more than just good common sense combined with some degree of technical competence. Apparently, it took a research scientist such as Fayol with a background in mining, engineering, and geology to recognize the importance of science in developing a better understanding of management.

Management is universal

The universality of management was noted earlier, but the concept is reemphasized at this point since it is an important consideration in contemporary management thought. Fayol suggested that managers should have the following attributes:

1. Physical qualities.
2. Mental qualities.
3. Moral qualities.
4. General Education.
5. Special knowledge related to specific operations.
6. Experience.

Practitioners often state that a study of management does not guarantee success as a manager. While this is true, five of the six attributes set forth by Fayol can be obtained to some degree through a formal study of management. Consequently, such study must not be taken lightly by those present and future mangers who wish to become more ware of their environment, the problems facing management, and the management techniques that may be used in improving organizational effectiveness.

If managers possess other abilities, they can become familiar with the unique features of a given organization while on the job. This point is highlighted in the Cudahy Packing Company's successful struggle for a comeback after near liquidation. After reorganization of the company, 11 of the 15 top-ranking officers were not only a new to Cudahy, but new to the meat industry as well. The president felt that these new managers could be taught the meat packing business since Cudahy needed the special expertise in marketing, finance, and personnel that these proven managers were able to provide. It should be remembered, however, that experience is not a good teacher unless one profits and learns in the process. Thus, experience often depends on the creation of situations that provide opportunities for learning.

Implied in the concept of universality is the idea that management skills and abilities are transferable from one organization to another. This viewpoint can be seen in the case of military officers who, upon retirement, may become excellent managers in other organizations. Of course, there are other cases where such transfers have not been successful. Earnest Dale casts doubt on the universality of management by suggesting that top-level executives of Standard Oil of New Jersey, the Roman Catholic Church, and the Communist Party are clearly not transferable. He further states that military personnel are chosen for industrial positions because of their value in securing military contracts, not because of their managerial expertise.

Although the movement from one management position to another says very little about the universality concept, questions can be raised. Are there key variables that permit the vice president of sales in a ball point pen company to move and become a successful executive in a steel manufacturing firm? Likewise, what makes it possible for a lawyer in the legal department of a large merchandising from to become an effective president of the same company? First, effective management depends on who well managers do their jobs: that is, how well they perform the management functions in seeking to accomplish predetermined objectives. Remember that the manager is no longer a specialist such as a lawyer, salesperson, engineer, or account, but a person who must plan, organize, actuate, and control. Again, this point does not deemphasize the importance of employing certain specialized knowledge in the decision making process. In this respect, technological, social, political, and economic factors must always must recognize the importance of balancing the needs and goals of all organization members. For top-level managers, however, these activities require an ability to see the overall picture of an organization's operations. When technical knowledge and information are required, staff personnel or outside consultants are available to provide such inputs.

The second factor to consider in the universality concept concerns the need for flexibility when adjusting to new organizational environments. Each organization has a different environment; and, for a manager to be effective in moving from one organization to another, he or she must be capable of adapting to change. In addition, the personal characteristics of initiative, motivation to achieve, and the courage to accept and overcome defeats and setbacks are also important. Max L. Cohen, president of Dino Boutiques, a major manufacturer of women's wear, states that a manager has to have drive and motivation—that is, "egoism and a natural biological drive." Successful managers, he feels, must have a love for the business and an unwillingness to let anyone down. Maurice Saltzman, president of Bobbie Brooks, Inc., puts his successful management career and life this way: "I can't wait until I get to the office the morning. I'm at the office every morning at 7:30 and stay until about 7:00 in the evening. I have a burning ambition to succeed. I've got to be a success at everything every day.

The requisites for the successful transferability of managers between organizations are also applicable to managerial promotions within the same organization. Success in all new managerial positions depends on a performance of the management functions: however, the intensity and direction of these functions change among the various level of management. As an example, planning often becomes relatively more important at the top-management level than at lower levels. Yet, regardless of how the importance of a given function may vary, one should remember that each manager must perform all of the management functions in seeking to accomplish established organizational objectives.

The evolution of approaches to management

During the past 50 years, social political, economic, and technical changes have had a tremendous impact on the practice of management. Through a scientific approach to problem solving, more managers have developed the ability to understand causal relationships between organizational phenomenon. Within the United States, the first major steps in this direction were taken by Frederick W. Taylor. Taylor and his followers sought ways to cut costs, improve efficiency, and measure the performance of workers by developing the best method for performing a job and then selecting the most qualified workers for the job. Through his experimentation, testing, and writing, Taylor became known as the "father" of the movement referred to as scientific management.

In the 1920s and 1930s, the emphasis of management study shifted to a more scientific examination of human beings in organizational settings. The study of interrelationships between people and work environments resulted in a new field of management called human relations. Pioneers, such as Elton Mayo and F.J. Roethlisberger, were among the first to be involved in extensive research efforts directed toward a better understanding of human behavior in the work situation. Since the 1930s, of course, contributions from areas such as psychology, sociology, and anthropology, have added significantly to the behavioral orientation of modern managers.

During the 1950s, other systematic approaches to the study and practice of management began to develop. All of these approaches encompass, to some degree, the common element of models and quantitative methods of analysis. For example, the use of statistics and mathematics in the decision-making process is now referred to as the field or management science. Even more recently, comparative management and general systems theory have developed as additional approaches to the study of management. Briefly, systems theory embodies the idea that an organization is an open-ended system of many parts. By properly recognizing the relationships between individual parts and the whole, as well as the influences of the external environment, overall objectives can be achieved more effectively. In general, comparative management attempts to provide an analysis of general management theory across various cultures, professions, and disciplines.

The diversity of approaches to the study of management has resulted in one author categorizing or grouping them "schools" of management thought. A brief description of these approaches to management can provide some idea about the extensiveness of management theories.

The prevalent views can be classified as:

1. *Empirical*—further the understanding of management techniques by comparing past experiences of managerial situations.
2. *Human behavioral*—integrating people into a

work environment that facilitates cooperation, creativity, and productivity.

3. *Social systems*—viewing management as a system of cultural interrelationships between people and as members of groups.
4. *Decision making*—understanding the who, why, and how of decision making by rationally weighing alternative courses of action through techniques in areas such as statistics and economics.
5. *Quantitative methods*—solving management problems through mathematical formuli and models.
6. *Systems management*—interrelating of parts to the over-all unit by recognizing inputs, processes, and output in order to optimize total objectives.
7. *Process*—achieving goals with people by performing the functions of planning, organizing, actuating, and controlling.

Although these approaches represent specific avenues to the study of management, they all reveal certain truths about the field. To a large extent, they actually provide support to, and act as tools for, managers in the complex environment of modern decision making. Thus, if managers consider only one of the approaches as being viable, they may actually hinder their success in decision making. Since modern managers deal with a variety of environmental influences and organizational inputs, they may find that a variety of viewpoints are essential in the practice of management. In reality, managers use classical management concepts as a framework for producing effective managerial actions. Through other insights, they are able to utilize knowledge about human behavior in the work environment. Finally, they can employ mathematical and quantitative techniques in the form of models that will contribute to more effective decision making. In this sense, the attempt is to find the most satisfactory decision, consistent with the constraints within which the manager must operate.

The art and science of management

The successful practice of management goes beyond applications of the scientific method of problem solving. An appropriate application of relevant knowledge depends on the skills and abilities of individual managers and may be referred to as the art of management. An artful practice of management depends upon innovative, creative, technical, human, and conceptual attributes of managers and is just as essential in the achievement of coordination as the science of management. R.L. Katz suggests that in bringing about desired results, we should consider the skills and abilities used by managers that can be developed and improved in applying management knowledge. He classifies the skills as (1) technical—the vocationally-obtained specialization of labor, (2) human—the ability to work with people versus the technical sill of working with things and processes, and (3) conceptual—the ability to recognize the interrelations and interconnections of the parts of an organization in the achievement of total organizational goals.

There is no doubt that the science and art of management must go hand in hand since one without the other is of little value to the practicing manager. One way to examine this point is to think about the medical doctor who performs delicate operations skillfully. Such skill, however, is based on a vast amount of knowledge provided by the study of chemistry, biology, anatomy, and physics.

Management education

The over-riding question about most educational courses and programmes is how good they are in academic terms. This question is asked by various validating bodies such as university Senates, the Council for National Academic Awards (CNAA), the American Association of Collegiate Schools of Business (AACSB), and so on. It is the price that must be paid if these bodies are to set their seals of approval behind such courses, and therefore make them viable products in the competitive world of management education. The greatest scrutiny normally takes place when a new course is being proposed. Proposers must be able to demonstrate that the syllabus conforms to that prescribed by the body in question: that the appropriate number of contact hours will be achieved in each area; that assessment procedures will be able to demonstrate without ambiguity that students have attained the appropriate levels;that the institution can provide sufficient facilities and resources to mount the programme; that the staff likely to be teaching on the programme have sufficient levels of experience and qualifications, and so on.

These are largely bureaucratic details which are extracted *before* the course is actually run in order to guarantee reasonable conformity and uniformity across that particular part of the educational system. The validation procedure tends to be considerably more rigorous in the USA than in the UK, and as a general principle it becomes *less* rigorous the further one moves up the ladder of educational qualifications. Therefore in the UK, for the time being, there is no syllabus whatsoever prescribed for students, but reasonably detailed syllabuses, and so on, are required for taught masters courses at universities; and the required detail increases for undergraduate courses at universities or for taught masters courses at polytechnics (CNAA validated).

Once the relevant validating body has pronounced the design of the educational product as satisfactory, the teachers concerned with the course are then left reasonably free to get on and run it. The validating bodies take very little interest in evaluating such programmes, and the question of Quality control is left to external examiners, who may occasionally be asked to submit reports on the course to the validating body. Provided there are no complaints from those involved, and the course does not have the misfortune to attract adverse political comment it may continue for many years without any further outside interest being taken.

Therefore there is not much external incentive for teachers in their institutions to take a very great interest in evaluation of their own courses. For the institutions there is a always the danger of creating unwelcome publicity; additionally for individual teachers, there are rarely any rewards either for good teaching or for taking additional interest in the teaching process. Nevertheless, there are still some hardy souls who persist with being interested in educational processes, and therefore the *subsidiary* questions that may be asked about educational courses and programmes are often around how enjoyable, how valuable; or how well taught a particular course has been.

I intend to provide three brief examples of evaluations of courses; these will mainly be in the area of student feedback, often initiated by the teachers involved. It seems difficult to find an example of evaluation carried out by a validating body, at least in the sense that I have been using the word 'evaluation' up to this point. In passing,however, I might offer some gratuitous advice about course submission to validating bodies. Four points here are:

1 provide sufficient details of the course and syllabus, but ensure that this is expressed clearly and simply;

2 be extremely careful to ensure that the

rubrics, structures, and logic of assessment are correct;

3 make sure that any external examiners involved are seen as respectable;

4 and go and talk to the officials who will be involved in vetting the proposal if you feel there are any unusual features involved.

The first genuine example of course evaluation comes from a fairly typical example of a student feedback questionnaire used in a leading North American business school and as can be seen from some of the sample questions in Figure 8.1 it is based entirely on multiple choice responses. These questionnaires are filled in anonymously by students at the end of each semester and are collected and analysed by the administration. It should be clear from the sampled questions that this instrument is basically concerned with *proving* and with forming judgments about the quality of each teacher's performance. The results of these questionnaires are not normally made public although they are said to be used in decisions about promotions and awarding tenure to members of the faculty. There is, however, a little skepticism about just how much notice is taken of this kind of information in actual decisions, since some of the more senior professors in the university are reputed to receive consistently low ratings from this instrument. Not only is there some doubt therefore about whether this instrument is really used for *proving* except perhaps in a few exceptional cases where evidence needs to be brought against people; but it is also of limited value in indicating to the teacher how he/she might actually *improve* his teaching performance.

Of slightly more use, particularly since they are intended for teaching development, are some of the feedback questionnaires employed in British universities and polytechnics. The example given in Figure 8.2 is taken from questionnaires used at the North East London Polytechnic. This uses relatively simple Likert-type questions which concentrate on what the lecturer seems to be doing and how he or she handles the relationship with students on the course. In this questionnaire there is no attempt to provide a judgement of the lecturer's overall performance; but the data provided by students of their experience of different aspects of the course should provide the lecturer with some pointers about the areas that might most constructively be worked upon should he or she wish to make some improvements.

A third example is of a number of studies that have been carried out in the Centre for the Study of Management Learning, University of Lancaster, with a view to improving the quality of some of the postgraduate courses being offered. One approach is to ask students.

Students carrying out evaluations of courses may find it of use to themselves to reflect upon how much, and what, they have derived from the course; they also seen interested in comparing such outcomes for themselves with those of their colleagues on the course. Since in most cases, they will be very unlikely to follow the same course again, they may be somewhat less interested in evaluative questions directed to *improving* future courses. That is why it is often easier for evaluations of educational programmes aimed at *improving* to be conducted by staff of the institutions concerned, but preferably not by the tutors and lecturers who may have gained their commitment to early models of the course. We have therefore found that the most useful evaluations aimed at this purpose are conducted along naturalistic lines, and by insider not directly involved with that particular course. Open-ended questionnaires or interviews seem to work best where they concentrate on questions such as:

- What did you like/dislike most about this course?
- What aspects of the course did you find most helpful/less helpful in contributing to your learning?
- What advice would you give to new students joining this course next year about how they can ensure that they are making the most of their opportunities?
- What are the three most important changes that could be made to this course in order to make it better in the future?

Although it is sometimes possible for tutors to talk over these matters with students, there may be some inhibitions on either side if the tutor has been closely involved in teaching on the course. Therefore it does seem easier for a relative outsider to take this role, and also to take responsibility for collating results, extracting themes and issues, and providing feed-back of overall results and conclusions to all those who participated in the study. Studies carried out at Lancaster on the postgraduate research programme have highlighted the need to provide more effective support between students; and occasional difficulties encountered in relationships between students and supervisors have resulted in slightly closer monitoring of supervisor/student relationships in general. These are a couple of improvements that have been made to the postgraduate research programme as a result of evaluation studies; other changes have been made in the case of several of the Centre's other programmes in order to deal with different issues and problems identified in this way.

Management training

The main interest here concerns the extent to which training courses can actually be used by those who attend them, and whether they are of relevance to the needs of these individuals, or to the needs of the organisations that have sponsored them. This contrasts somewhat with the interest in maintaining academic standards and quality; which has predominated in the context of educational courses and programmes - but perhaps it should still be noted that both maintain a primary focus on *outcomes*.

Evaluations of these programmes are conducted or initiated by the institution itself, since most training establishments are slightly more independent from outside control and validation than are educational institutions. Here I am referring to *educational* controls. Many training establishments will be subjected to tighter *financial* controls then educational establishments. But in most cases it is not at all clear what purpose is to be served by such evaluations, and there seems to be a large element of 'ritual' in the case of management training.

One of the most common rituals is the short (two page) questionnaire which is distributed at the end of a course, and sometimes at key points during the course. The questionnaires may be open or closed. Of the two, closed formats are rather more common when used in the middle of a course because they take less time to complete and can be easily computed into indices which can provide clear indications of ups and downs in the course, more-or-less as they are happening. The focus of such questionnaires is normally on the *inputs*; and with end of course questionnaires there are usually a few items to cover administrative aspects.

This form of evaluation is regarded as something of a ritual by people at both ends of the process. The questionnaire illustrated above might be thought of as aimed at *proving*, but this is not really the case since the results produced are rarely taken as anything more than diagnostic. Provided that the ratings are reasonably high in comparison with similar programmes, no action needs to be taken. if any of them drop below what is considered to be an acceptable level, this may indicate that some remedial action is necessary, such as changing the course or the teacher involved. In this respect, therefore, the real purpose of such routine evaluation may in a way be regarded as *improving*.

From time to time, institutions decide to conduct 'in depth' studies of a particular course or programme; these often require considerable resourcing, often from outside experts. Since additional funding is normally involved, the studies tend to have far higher visibility than routine evaluation work, and therefore it is almost inevitable that they will be drawn into the political arena. Such political implications may relate to the reasons for commissioning a study in the first place to the kinds of questions that different people would like to have answered, or to the kinds of answers they would like to receive to those questions. Two examples of such studies will be presented in the remainder of this section, and some of the political problems involved will be highlighted.

Example 1

The first example is a study of a junior management course carried out for the staff college of an important public sector organisation in the UK, and which was conducted by myself and two colleagues on a part-time basis over about four months. The main question asked of us was whether was considered this particular course to be meeting the current and future needs of the business, and whether there were changes that could be made to the course in order to strengthen its relevance. Behind this question we were also aware from other sources in the company that top management had been asking some pointed questions about the value of the staff college, and there was therefore the possibility of significant reorganizations being introduced in the near future. Nevertheless, in the meantime our clients were the senior tutorial staff in the college itself.

The remit given to us the clients suggested that our primary focus should be on the organizational *context* from which managers attending the course had come - rather than on inputs and processes within the course itself. We therefore started talking to samples of managers, both those attending the current course and some who had attended similar courses several months previously about the nature of their jobs, what they found difficult about those jobs, what changes they were experiencing at the present time, and what kind of changes they anticipated in their areas of the business in the near future. Some of these talks were tape recorded, but the majority were recorded by the interviewer in note form, with direct quotations being taken down whenever they seemed to be of significance.

One particular interest of ours in this study was to extreme the perceptions of change in the business held by managers who had attended the course, and compare these with perceptions of change from managers who had not attended the course. A content analysis of the several dozen interviews conducted indicated that those managers who had attended the course were perceiving more of the broad changes taking place in the business, than those who had not attended. However, it was also evident that those managers who attended the course did have considerable difficulty relating their perceptions of what was going on in their own *immediate* work environment to the material that was introduced on the course. This was indicated by the fact that there was no difference in perceptions at this level, between those who had, and those who had not, attended the course. One of the principles in the 'transfer' of training is that managers should be able to relate materials on the course to contexts where each manager has some degree of control, and in this respect the course did not seem to be succeeding. Consequently one of our main recommendations was about ways of 'grounding' the material and content of the course in the experiences of individual managers through making use of methods such as projects, individualised case studies, and action learning sets.

Another problem about this example was that we were already well embarked upon the project when we realised a fundamental flaw in our design: we had been asked to look at whether the *course* was meeting the needs of the business, but we were asked specifically not to observe any of the course sessions in practice. We therefore had to make do with second-hand information about the process of formal sessions on each course which was provided by participants and tutors. The need to piece together indirect evidence occasionally placed us in a rather insecure position and, although we were eventually reasonably confident that we knew what it was that we had not observed, the absence of direct access did create an additional problem.

The results of this study were written up and delivered in a form which was closest to the predominant culture of the company, and they were presented on time! the only additional problem by this stage of the study was that both of the vital clients who had been instrumental in commissioning the study had been moved on to new jobs elsewhere in the company. Although these individuals had formally been replaced, the main commitment that had been generated for making use of the results was therefore lost. Many of our recommendations were also superseded by a significant reorganisation of the training function which followed soon after, and we were only able to hope that some of them had been quietly assimilated into the new arrangements.

Example 2

The above example may be taken as a cautionary tale about the importance of maintaining good links with vital clients and sponsors during the evaluation study when one is an outsider to the organisation is question. Above all, one should try to discourage clients from being moved or reorganised during the period of the study. The second example, which follows, also encountered some problems with clients, although these were less drastic, and it was therefore possible to accommodate them adequately within the aims of the study. Another interesting feature of the case was that it was necessary to change the evaluation design quite significantly as the study progressed; the earlier part being close to the experimental research school of thought, and the latter part adopting much more of an interventionalist model. The course which was the subject of the evaluation was run on a part-time basis over a period of twelve months for a group of training officers from an Industrial Training Board The Training Board sponsored the participants and the course was run by a university business school. The main question posed at the outset by the Programme Director was whether the course had any effect on the way the training officers went about their jobs. Therefore a short multiple choice questionnaire was administered before the start of the programme to all prospective participants, including some who did not eventually come on the course. The questionnaire was intended to measure how they currently saw their jobs, and their attitudes towards the work involved in these job. These questionnaires were complemented by two types of repertory grid the first using a set of elements such as 'Myself as I am', 'A Progressive Manager', 'An Effective Trainer', and so on from which about six constructs were derived using the normal trading method; the second type of grid involved asking the training officers to define a set of elements based on what they experienced as the main problems in their jobs, and then deriving through the interview a set of constructs which expressed how they typically tried to cope with each of these problems.

Some of the information, especially that provided by the latter of the two repertory grids, was provided to the Course Director before the programme started in order to help him adapt the content and design to the needs of the group that he was likely to be encountering.

After this initial burst of data collecting activity, I maintained a low profile in this course, occasionally visiting it while residential sessions were being held, and chatting informally to participants in the bar, but not attending any of the formal sessions. Brief 'Reactions Sheets' were distributed by the Course Director at the end of each module, and these were collected up and collated by himself and a secretary. My next major involvement with the programme began about one month before the final week, when I telephoned the Course Director to discuss arrangements for the final phase of data collection, and for the presentation of evaluation results at the final review meeting. During this conversation he mentioned to me that the manager in the Training Board who had been given liaison responsibility for this programme was coming under some internal pressure, and that he would be most interested to know a little more about how the programme was going. It was at this point that the evaluation study began to change from the experimental research to the interventioalist 'school of thought'.

We telephoned the manager concerned, to tell him how things were going, and at the same time I decided to ask him about the kind of information that he was hoping the evaluation might produce. His immediate response was that he hoped that it would 'break through the fogs about what it is that the training officers say they are getting out of this programme'. He also added that perhaps I should ask his other colleagues in the Training Board, who had nominated individual training officers from their areas to come on this course, what they were expecting their nominees to get from the course, and to what extent they felt this had been achieved.

There are three main aspects of this development. Firstly, by asking the manager what *he* was expecting from the evaluation, we were acknowledging that the Course Director was not the sole client for the evaluation. Other people clearly felt they had a stake in it, and it therefore became necessary to try to accommodate their needs too. Secondly, by accepting a wider definition of the client group, we were being influenced to look for things other than those specified in the formal aims of the course, or in the original design of evaluation. The third aspect was that we were thereby starting to become involved in the politics of the Training Board. The manager with liaison responsibility was evidently coming under some pressure from his colleagues to justify expenditure on this programme. Perhaps one way of countering some of this pressure was to send an "evaluator' around to them to ask precisely what they expected their own training officers to obtain from the course - and these were questions which the manager knew his colleagues would have difficulty in answering.

I had now committed myself to spend additional time travelling around the country meeting managers in various areas of the Board's operation. Due to the deeper involvement with the sponsoring organisation, my interviews with participants towards the end of the programme were considerable broader than simply asking them to complete the pre-course instruments once again.

As a result of these broader interviews it was possible to identify a number of particular issues which had an important impact upon the way this particular course ran, and some of which would have a bearing upon the designs of subsequent courses. Some resulting issues were:

1. Senior management appeared to be exceedingly unclear about why they were sponsoring this programme, and what they believed the training officers should be getting out of it.
2. The initial meetings of participants in small groups with the Course Director and evaluator

before the course began were experienced by some as 'traumatic'. They commented that in discussions with the Course Director they felt they were being sold a product and that they would virtually have no opportunity to influence what went into the programme; they also disliked being asked to complete the pre-course evaluation instruments.

3. Some parts of the programme were regarded as markedly less successful than others, and an important factor in this was the degree of commitment that each tutor appeared to be making to the course.
4. The 'project' part of the course was crucial to the overall success for each participant. If the choice of project was a 'good' one the overall experience was positive; but if the project turned out to be unsuccessful, this rather soured the experience of the whole course.

In the discussion at the end of the course about the evaluation report, it was the description of some of the issues arising which created by far the most interest. Not only did these provide answers to some of the questions that people had asked, they were also able to recognise some of their own contributions to understanding what had taken place. The more quantitative results of the attitude surveys and repertory grids were noted, but they did not create much interest, partly because they were addressed to questions which were only of marginal interest to those involved (*proving*), and partly because they had been manipulated statistically in order to provide conclusions. Since participants and others could not see clearly the link between the information they had provided and the conclusions that were drawn from that information, this material therefore had relatively low face validity.

Three items can be highlighted from the two examples described in some detail above. Firstly in the evaluation of management training courses it is invariably essential to clarify precisely who is, or are, the client(s), and to find out what it is that they want to know. Not only do such clients control the purse-strings, they are also the only people who are really in a position to do anything with the results of the study. One needs to be wary of this. Secondly in both of these examples I found it rather difficult to get close to the actual *process* of the courses, and had to make do with second-hand reports - the piecing together of these reports often seemed to take more time than direct observation of sessions would have required, and as an observer I would have been more confident about my observations. Therefore in similar cases it might be worth ensuring that when negotiating contracts for such a study, questions about access to 'the real thing' should also be negotiated and agreed at the outset. Thirdly in both cases I found that *naturalistic* interviews were far more useful than more structured forms of data collection - perhaps because of the complexity of what was being investigated, and the need therefore to maintain flexibility over one's design and focus. The main problem, of course, with such methods is that they are excessively time-consuming, and they require a fairly high degree of skill on the part of the interviewer. If this kind of 'useful' evaluation is to be employed widely, there is therefore an urgent need to streamline and automate these naturalistic data collection procedures.

Management development

In this section I shall try to cover both the organisation-wide systems aimed primarily at the development of an *individual* manager, and the programmes or interventions which are ostensibly aimed at improving the functioning of groups, or the organisation as a whole. As far as evaluation is concerned, much of the work in these area has been of a pragmatic nature with an emphasis on *improving*, although, particularly in the case of organisation development, there have been a number of rather traditional research studies aimed at *proving* the value of an intervention. Where evaluation has been carried out, this has been assumed to be primarily for the benefit of personnel specialists and senior management, although there are examples of wider client groups being acknowledged, especially when the democratic values of an OD intervention managed to be translated into the practice of its evaluation. I shall start by discussing the evaluation of OD interventions, before returning to a consideration of systems aimed primarily at the development of *individuals*.

Methodologically there are two distinct

traditions in OD. Firstly there are a number of case studies of single interventions which in most cases have been written up by the consultants themselves who managed those interventions. Apart from the obvious commercial advantages for consultants who are able to publish 'respectable' evidence of the success of their own interventions, there is also a strong tradition of action research in this area which leads rather naturally to such self-evaluations. This action research often forms a crucial part of an OD intervention, and usually involves some form of data collection in the organisation, feedback of that data to a wide range of interested parties, and some form of resultant action planning. Action research generally works better when the managers, who are themselves the objects of the study, also participate quite extensively in carrying out the study; hence the tendency noted above for client groups to become quite wide in a number of instances. French and Bell, summarise these two traditions neatly in relation to action research:

Two philosophical and pragmatic values underlie action research. The first value is that action plans and programmes designed to solve real problems should be based on valid public data generated collaboratively by clients and consultants. This belief calls for action to be based on diagnostic research - *and action should follow research...* The second value is that action in the real world should be accompanied by research on that action so that we can build up an accumulative body of knowledge and theory of the effects of various action directed to solving a real world problem a *research should follow action* mode of thinking.

The second tradition is markedly different in function, and the emphasis on accumulation of knowledge tends to lead to distinct methods being employed also. Frequently these take the form of traditional research methods employing multiple-choice questionnaires to survey large numbers of managers and employees in order to identify whether changes have taken place across the organsation as a result of OD interventions or the operation of management development systems. This survey data is often backed up by statistics on organisational performance, and occasionally by interview data. However, it is rare to find the subjects of such survey involved in interpreting survey results - as they might well do in the first tradition.

One of the reasons for the diversity of evaluation practice is the complexity of conducting work in this area. At least five problems can be noted. Firstly, it is by no means easy to agree on the conceptual boundaries of what is to be investigated. There is enormous variation in the practice of management and organisation development, and each contains a wide variety of philosophies, value systems, techniques, and structures. Secondly there are practical problems of defining boundaries when evaluating techniques and procedures that supposedly cover complete organisations. This may not be too difficult in an organisation, or sub-unit, employing a few hundred people; but poses sever limitations when the organisation employs several hundred thousand people. Thirdly, evaluation of programmes and systems frequently has implications for the politicians for the politics of the organisation. People's job and careers may be closely linked to the success or failure of the management development programmes that they are promoting or sponsoring. Since the information can be a very potent political weapon, the generation of information through evaluation may well be used to support the views and interests of those who control its dissemination. Fifthly, when OD methods are being used, it may be exceedingly difficult to distinguish between actions undertaken as part of the intervention, and research conducted as part of the evaluation. As in the hallowed tradition of the Hawthorne study, both action and evaluation may have significant, and unpredictable effects on their subjects.

There is an enormous range of published literature about organisation development, including numerous evaluation studies which have attempted to assess whether or not it works. French and Bell cite a number of papers, each of which reviews the results of dozens of individual studies. But which, collectively, do not lead to any definitive conclusion. But it is worth emphasising a couple of points made by French and Bell with regard to these evaluation studies. Firstly, they note a trend towards more rigidly controlled and comparative research designs which make use of independent evaluators, a trend they are strongly in support of. Secondly, they regard the scarcity of acceptable theory - about how any why OD works or does not work - as a major hindrance to the establishment of definitive results about the effects of OD. My comment on this, from an evaluation perspective, is that there may be a contradiction between French and Bell's two points, and perhaps they would be advised to focus more on *processes* with a view to *improving* OD, before returning to the quest for *proof* with its consequent concentration upon *outcomes*.

4 Scientific Management and Technology

The traditional approach to the problems of management was to tackle these as they arose. No attempt was made to anticipate them or to make advance provision for meeting them. Management was accepted to be an art for which an inbred flair was needed. This allowed one to cope with any eventuality by the use of such resources as were available at the time. When it became evident that a common approach to frequently recurring problems was an advantage, a systematic procedure was instituted to ensure uniformity in dealing with similar circumstances on different occasions. Examples have been given in earlier chapters of systematic procedures in management practice in relation to some of the topics already considered. Occasional reference has also been made to the findings of investigators who have looked into various situations in an effort to lay bare the underlying truths. This is an improvement on a mere systematic approach, as it leads to the creation of new knowledge and is more effective than the procedure of continuing to use a system uncritically. Since it is built upon successful practice, systematic procedure is likely to be effective, but only in relation to certain conditions. A better method of working can be discovered only by deliberate investigations that seek information on which better ideas can be based.

Scientific method is a logical procedure of observation, reasoning and the formulation of ideas. The aim is to discover the truth concerning a given situation. This is done by gathering together all the discernible facts, classifying them, and attempting to arrive at their meaning by the application of the principles of logical reasoning. The five steps of the scientific method are:

(1) Observation of the phenomena under investigation;

(2) The hypothesis—the formulation of theories based on the observed facts;

(3) Experimentation—designed to test the theories evolved;

(4) Determination of the general law by comparison of the experimental results with the results predicted by the theories;

(5) Use of the general law in particular cases.

In the application of the scientific method to management the first two steps are always relatively easy. Facts can be observed and an idea then formulated that fits the facts. The experimentation carried out may be only to test the validity of alternative solutions to the problem posed, so that the correct one is found for use in the circumstances. The weakness of this application of the scientific method is the difficulty of proving the validity of the theories postulated by undertaking supporting experiments in different companies and under altered working conditions. There is, accordingly, a tremendous amount of duplication and wasted effort, as each company is seeking new ideas by observation and experimentation, but only within its own prescribed circumstances and conditions.

An example of an application of science in management illustrates the first two steps of observation and formulation. In the production of knitted fabrics for women's cardigans it was noticed that the wastage caused by scrap in processing tended to fluctuate considerably for no apparent reason. First of all it was necessary to determine the factors that could have a bearing upon the wastage. Obviously the type of damage causing the rejection of the fabric could be classified to provide an indication but, apart from this, six other possible causes were identified by investigation. These were yarn size, yarn regularity, yarn tension, machine speed and the temperature and humidity of work-rooms. Observations then had to be made over a period of time to find out which of these was the real or main cause. Statistical diagrams were used to reveal correlation by plotting weekly variations of all the possible causes. A careful study of the results showed that the periods of considerable damage to the knitted fabric were also periods of low humidity. Although the knitting room had been temperature controlled, no attempt had been made to maintain constant humidity. The theory arrived at was that with the installation of a humidifying plant the incidence of damage would fall to a steady level much below that experienced in the past.

In such a situation it is not always possible to try out the solution on an experimental basis. A small-scale pilot scheme can sometimes be introduced but this is not always feasible. The application by the manager of theories evolved by scientific investigation of management problems may have to proceed as an act of faith in the ability of the scientist guiding him. Unfortunately, there are likely to be side effects to the introduction of new ideas and fresh methods of working that cannot be foreseen in the absence of experimentation, and it is through troubles arising from such unfortunate experiences that the application of scientific management has sometimes been discredited.

Contributions of the pioneers

Many of the pioneers of the application of science to management have already been referred to in earlier chapters without any indication that they were concerned with scientific methods. Adam Smith, a professor of logic and moral philosophy, laid the foundation for the science of economics in his book *An Inquiry into the Nature and Causes of the Wealth of Nations*. The principal contribution he made to manufacturing activity was the identification, from observation, of the advantages of the division of labour, with its attendant increase of productivity.

Charles Babbage, after a brilliant career as a scientist, including an appointment as Professor of Mathematics at Cambridge, pointed out the possibility of developing general principles, based on the use of scientific method, to govern the conduct of industrial undertakings. His analysis of processes in pin making followed Adam Smith's line of reasoning, but he also attached scientifically determined details of the time and cost, which permitted the calculation of the cost of making each pin to units of a millionth of a penny. His identification of the importance of balance of processes was of great importance to later attempts at mass production. From the economic standpoint he also laid foundations for the scientific determination of the best size of the manufacturing unit.

The Frenchman Fayol was also a successful manager who, on looking back over his long career in a top management position, applied the logical approach to the enunciation of the principles by which he had gained his success. His analysis of the groups of operations found in business, his principles and administrative duties, his identification of the qualities needed in the manager, were all succinctly expressed yet they embodied a wealth of wisdom that has provided a basic guide to managers for generations.

The American who is the accredited "father" of scientific management is F.W. Taylor. His insistence on the abandonment of military types of line organisation and their replacement by functional management was one of his contributions. The division of the responsibilities of supervisors, leading to functional foremanship, has been referred to earlier. Taylor insisted on the importance of scientific investigation and experimental method as a better alternative than the then prevailing traditional methods of management. He identified as a characteristic of scientific management a "complete mental revolution" on the part of both workers and managers. This was an advocacy of harmony and co-operation by combined efforts instead of a perpetuation of the division between capital and labour. From the realisation of the importance of relating monetary rewards to work done, Taylor's work laid the foundation for the association of scientific management and incentives. He showed that it was possible to combine high wages and low labour costs for each job by assigning to the workers a large daily task to be performed under standard condition with a high pay reward for successful completion, and loss to the worker if he failed. As an example of the successful application of the scientific method of working he had evolved. Taylor quotes an increase in the tonnage of pig iron handled from 12 1/2 to 47 tone per day with the same labour force. However, when other managers tried to apply Taylor's ideas, without also having his central philosophy as a guide, antagonism rather than harmony resulted from the application of scientific methods of working.

This antagonism did not however, constitute general criticism of the validity of the methods so much as signify opposition to the way changes had been imposed. The scientific application did not embrace the human element.

There were, however, two later contributors to the knowledge of the method of applying science to management who were contemporaries and both concerned with substantially the same type of application to the human aspect of the working situation. The psychologist Mary Parker Follet applies the findings of the social sciences to industry and evolved a new concept of human relations within groups of people at work. She advocated the application of scientific method to management and suggested the use of the knowledge in all the sciences, particularly psychology and anthropology. The idea that dominated her thought was wholeness as expressed by the integration and co-ordination of the ever-changing forces implicit in management. Her contemporary was B.S. Rowntree, renowned for his sociological investigations but an industrialist by vocation. His main contribution was to show the way in which scientific methods could be applied to the human factor. He implemented a system of democracy in industry, complete with joint consultation and disciplinary appeals machinery, but he rejected the idea of paternalism or welfare for its own sake. His work at his family's chocolate factory at York was not confined to the application of science in the personnel division of the company, he also instituted a scientific study of the sales and clerical organisations.

These brief biographical notes on some of the foremost of those associated with the application of science show the many fields of endeavour from which such people have come. University professors, practising managers, engineers, psychologists, these and others have all played some part in showing how fact can replace opinion when scientific management is applied. They were all scientists or technologists, and highly trained in their own professions before turning to the management activities they helped to improve, but this does not imply that only such person can usefully engage in scientific management. It is possible, in practice, for the logical procedure of observation, for reasoning, and for the exposition of ideas to be put into a step-by-step framework that can be used by practical men who are neither academics nor technologists.

Features of scientific management.

Having described the scientific method and seen something of the results of its use by many people, it is now possible to bring together some of the common features of their work so that the general nature of scientific management becomes apparent. The feature immediately evident is that of the application of the scientific method to management. This involves the substitution of scientific investigation, with the resultant revelation of fact for the older judgment or opinion. This attitude may be thought of as the guiding philosophy from which all else springs. It is a big step towards effective operations when all managers adopt this philosophy. The outcome of its application will be to look ahead so that plans can be laid for the future—a direct opposite of the traditional method of waiting until the occurrence and then arriving at a solution by "hunch". The separation of planning from performance was seen to be an integral part of Taylor's functional foremanship and is an incidental feature of scientific management generally.

When the future is predictable and detailed planning can precede performance, it is possible to set scientifically determined standards as criteria for an activity, so that comparisons can be made to reveal the adequacy and effectiveness of the performance desired. Scientific management is concerned with improvements based on detailed knowledge of past events. The predetermined standards for comparison are essential to this knowledge, but it is also necessary to compile records. The information need for comparisons must be recorded to provide the basis for future plans and standards. The comparisons made in such records can be used also to show ineffectiveness, so that the attention of operating managers is drawn to a factual basis for improvement. Fayol described this as "seeing that everything occurs in conformity with established rule and expressed command" whereas Brech refers to control as "the checking of achievement against plans". In referring to the growing extent of the factual basis for management decisions, Mary Parker Follett said:

"control is coming more and more to mean fact-control rather than man control".

Control therefore now has an especial meaning for managers in the sense that it provides the facts from which continued efficiency can spring. The revolution of thinking that accompanies scientific management leads to unification of the interests of all the participants in joint business activity. This altruistic aim may be encouraged by many devices that result from the application of science, but the greater monetary return to owners, managers and workers alike provides the main encouragement to harmony and expansion of the opportunities of all sections of industry.

The improvement of efficiency by scientific management is made possible by the maintenance of records, and also by harmony of working. When current utilisation of all resources is concentrated upon waste of all kinds, much that went undetected until facts were made available by scientific investigations will be eliminated. The avoidance of waste results in a lowering of the cost of manufacture, and this can be further accentuated by systematic investigation of all the activities of manufacture, distribution and management. Nothing should be shielded from investigation. Every aspect of the company should be open to scrutiny to ensure that it is contributing fully to the ultimate success of the joint effort. This emphasis on success and efficiency with its stress on the appropriate contribution of every part of the enterprise led, at one stage, to the use of the term "Efficiency Engineering" to describe the applications then being made of scientific management.

Benefits of scientific management.

Few people are so gullible as to be willing to pursue an idea unless they expect some beneficial result. This must be as true of scientific management as of anything else that affects people's lives. If there is to be a greater striving for efficiency, of what benefit is this going to be? If the worker is affected by this mental revolution, what will be the result for him? Rowntree's answer to these queries was to recognise scientific management as a means of achieving an ever-rising standard of living. This would affect not only the workers, but also the whole of society by the creation of more real wealth by the better utilisation of natural resources. Of more immediate concern within the company are such benefits as:

Reduction of labour trouble following the change in mental attitudes of both managers and men;

Higher productivity resulting, not from harder work, but from more effective workmanship;

Improvement of the quality of products following the institution of control procedures;

Prompt deliveries by effective planning and so the maintenance of customers' good will as well as surety of a steady income in return for goods despatched.

To the worker the following benefits should accrue:

Steady employment because plans have been made to give greater stability of activity for periods ahead;

High pay with easier work by the evolution of more effective methods of working;

Satisfaction at work, following the application of scientific selection procedures, and the motivation resulting from supervisors' work;

Improved working conditions, since attention will have been paid to the workers' physical and mental well-being.

Processes of scientific management

In the present state of development it is possible to isolate certain process that have resulted from the application of scientific method to the art of government in industrial and commercial undertakings. These stand alone and can be thought of as distinct process, but the extent to which this separation is possible in practice depends upon the size of the enterprise and the extent to which specialisation of management duties can be taken. The primary elements involved in the management process have been seen to be:

— to foresee by examining the future;

— to provide the means by drawing up the plan of action;

— building the dual structure, material and human;

— maintaining activity among personnel;

— binding together, unifying and harmonising all activity and effort;

— seeing that everything occurs in conformity with established rule and expressed command.

These are the elements that we present in management of a scientific nature, but to complete the list it is necessary to differentiate planning from forecasting as the two constituent parts of foresight, and also to change the word "command", with the implication of harsh discipline accompanied by sanctions, to the less severe "motivation", in line with the development of thought about the best way of encouraging an optimum contribution by each employee to the affairs of the company. There is thus a list of six activities that are generally recognised to be the management processes associated with the scientific approach. These processes are listed in the accompanying table, which also shows, in relation to each of them, what is involved in the application of each and its important characteristics. It will be seen that the processes have been grouped in pairs and associated with a particular category of administrator, or manager, who is invested with responsibility for the application and correct use of the processes in practice.

The suggestion that functional managers

exists as a separate category from line managers is a direct reflection of the extent to which specialisation follows the application of science to management. This is not to say that the processes of planning and control can be applied only be planning managers and controllers established solely for that purpose.

These are four of the processes of scientific management that are considered to be inherent in managers' duties, so that a manager imbued with the scientific approach to his job would be concerned with these in his job, no matter to what extent similar processes had been instituted elsewhere within the undertaking.

It is thus evident that there is a personal as well as an organisational aspect to the application of scientific management. It is not sufficient to have an appropriate organisation structure deliberately planned to enable the company to take advantage of scientific management processes; it is necessary, also, for all managers to adopt the elements of scientific management in their approach to their own jobs if they are to work with maximum effectiveness. This will prompt them to plan their own activities, and those of their team where this is not done by some system of planning, so that maximum use is made of the available time of all concerned. The manager will also co-ordinate his activities and inter-personal relations with colleagues, superiors, and subordinates, so that the resulting collective action ensures harmony of working to achieve the aims of the enterprise. He will motivate the persons for whose work he is held responsible, by inspiring them in the performance of their duties. Finally, he will frequently check their activities to ensure that what was expected of them has been achieved. In this way, it is seen that four of the processes of scientific management in action can also be absorbed into individual duties as the elements of management.

Developments

Since 1945 we have seen a second movement to the original scientific management" movement of the late 19th and early 20th centuries which has resulted in the rise of a true management technology, a body of concepts and techniques derived from the mathematical and other exact sciences and the behavioural science. If you are interested in tracing origins you might note that it has sometimes been attributed to the use of operational research in the conduct of World War II, while others have singled out Norbert Wiener's book *Cybernetics* as a milestone. Management sciences resort frequently to the use of models of business situations. Mathematical programming and simulation techniques may be applied to the construction of models of the operation of a company. A work study team will make a scale model of a factory or office layout, the better to study possible revisions. What management is doing is developing the analysis of tasks to specialists who can thus help in the choice of the most apt solutions.

Another feature has been the adoption of

mathematics as a discipline relevant to the solution of management and organisational problems. Mathematical sciences have been applied to project control, decision-making, quality control and strategic planning. We talk and write often of numeracy and the "numerate" manager.

Also typical of the new management technology is the inter-disciplinary team, which may include statistician, psychologist, econometrician, biologist, computer scientist, accountant, a selection of these specialist and others, as appropriate. A short book such as *New Thinking in Management* by F. de P. Hanika epitomises the development, although it is by no means the only book concerned with these matters. Its chapters are headed: a Systems View of Organisation, Characteristics of Business Organisation. Decision Theory, Information Theory, Simulation, Programming and Operational Research, Heuristic Methods, Organisation Analysis, Economic Analysis, and Operations Analysis, respectively. The new and sometimes formidable terminology which this typifies is one of the recognition marks of the new technology.

The behavioural sciences such as psychology, sociology and associated studies have come more into the picture. Their concern for the human beings in industry showed itself long ago in the now renowned Hawthorne Experiment of the 1920s and early 1930; the concern is now a very full study of behaviour at work in which research has proliferated.

Management is going to need these analytical techniques, this management science, even more widely in the future; there is inevitably some risk that preoccupation with them will form so great part of our day-to-day anxiety as even to obscure the nature of the fundamental managerial situation. Therefore creative thinking, initiative and maturity of judgment will become even more imperative needs. Nor can the exercise of skills in human relations be relaxed.

Management services

It is becoming common practice to group together a number of management and productivity techniques in a central management services unit, division or section at the headquarters of the group, the head of management services reporting direct to the chief executive of the enterprise. In some companies the unit has originated from an internal audit section, in others from Organisation and Methods, in others from the development of data processing. There are firms in which it was in effect inaugurated by a team of consultants carrying out an assignment in the company and staying on as the nucleus of management services.

Such divisions are subject to considerable variations of scope and of organisation structure; nothing like a standard pattern has yet imposed itself. However, some more or less general trends are discernible. For instance, the management services division will often be subdivided into three or four sections such as;

(a) Organisation and methods and clerical work measurement;

(b) Computer operations;

(c) Operational research;

(d) Work study.

While some departments are narrowly restricted to productivity services, others will range from these to corporate or strategic planning and investment appraisal. As a rule, however, whatever the composition of the unit, it will be expected to raise the efficiency of operation in the fields it investigates and to reduce costs where this is compatible with such greater efficiency. As to the techniques included, at least one writer has listed more than a hundred. Some of the following might be found in management services.

There are a number of reasons for assembling these far from homogeneous 'techniques in one centralised management services unit. First among these are the advantages to be gained from the concentration of a pool of specialised staff who can thus be of optimum mutual assistance in their various projects.

There is a tendency to centralise management information service, and the creation of a management services division helps considerably towards this end, especially where an integrated data processing unit is part of the division.

In some companies the unit can serve as a training ground for young executives who are expected to rise in the management team of the company and will benefit very much from a closer acquaintance with actual management techniques projects.

There is also a measure of administrative convenience in having a whole range of such technology made the responsibility of one head. This should lead to better control and reporting. There may well be certain economies to be secured by mutual servicing of the teams inside the unit.

This type of organisation also furthers the growth of the interdisciplinary project, itself very much a a development of which a great deal more will be heard in the immediate future. The typical management science assignment will be a group effort, with a number of disciplines or expertises applied to common aim by way of logic, and scientific and analytical method.

Nevertheless, as already stated, there is no standard practice. The arrangement adopted depends very much on decisions made.in the company itself about what fits their organisation best. Some of the services may be decentralised, particularly where a company or group of companies has a number of geographically separate establishments. For instance, it may then prefer to have a work study unit in each major plant, with such units reporting to a central management services division to which they are ultimately responsible.

At the other end of the scale, the small company will be unlikely to support a specialised full-time management services unit. There, one of the executives of the company might number among his functions the supervisions of projects such as a work measurement exercise or the introduction of a job evaluation scheme.

The scope of a management services unit is (a) to devise solutions and procedures to cope with specific problems and (b) on certain other matters to collect and process data for subsequent decision making by line management. Under (a) come the investigations of defined factory processes or office systems. There is functional objective; the management services team will contribute towards achieving it. Under (b) come quite different projects which involve a survey and analysis of the business organisation as a whole, looking on it for this purpose as an inter-connected and complex system of working. These are strategic exercises and the management science applied to them will often amount to a quantification of risk as a guide for the decision maker.

Whatever the type of project in hand, much of its success will hang on the association of line managers in the assignments given to management services. The definition of the problem given at the start of the exercise can be important. A management services unit is making recommendations; it is not ultimately responsible for decision making but it is for the calibre and viability of its advice and recommendations.

The method of management services is very much the scientific method mentioned elsewhere in this book. The team will make a start by probing the problem given to them; it is not unknown for management services to come up at this stage with so radically changed a statement of the real problem as to make it seem a very different one from that originally presented to them.

It will next try to establish the category into which the problem falls. What appeared at first acquaintance to be unique turns out to have parallels. One is referring here to the classification into such general groups as queueing, inventory, search, allocation, sequencing, maintenance and replacement and competitive strategy. Identification of the class of problem should lead to the selection of the appropriate management technique.

The team can now proceed to direct observation so that the relevant data can be collected, arranged and processed. Solution can then be formulated in detail and tested. The solution foused most acceptable will be recommended to management for their examination and decision. A generally accepted solution can then be implemented and the effects can be evaluated.

It is never such an easy sequence of events as appears above. To begin with the non-specialist and the line manager are apt to be aware of an element of mystique surrounding some of the management services techniques. The terminology is new. The quantitative analysis may be something to which they are not accustomed. Then there are a bewilderingly large number of techniques, some of which involve unusually large investment of time and effort. Communication between expert and line management may not be easy. Mistaken "do-it-yourself" attempts and the over-simplification of complex problems can even discredit management services altogether. Inside the unit itself there are other problems. How successful is one in recruiting and using the services of qualified and experienced staff? Systems analysts, corporate planners, specialists in investment appraisal, econometricians—some of these are bound to be in short supply. As regards the actual projects themselves, even the best recommendations still face the hurdle of acceptability: line management is not always longing to be convinced of the value of change.

The planning of the departmental programme of assignments and projects is only too often a matter of stretching manpower and other resources to the limit. From the point of view of general management the unit can itself appear to be a costly one; it will be staffed largely by highly trained specialists.

We have said that some techniques are directed primarily at the improvement of selected systems and procedures or the productivity of a stated division; others are more directly related to the strategy of the whole company.

The first category, which is probably more generally recognised as particularly the area of management services, includes Organisation and

Methods, work study, the various forms of network analysis and critical path planning, systems analysis, value analysis and ergonomics, among others.

The second includes corporate planning, capital investment appraisal, management information systems and economic forecasting. It is in these strategic fields that the availability of computer facilities makes it feasible to construct fuller models of an enterprise and to study the pattern of a large and complex business in action. Even the small company cannot take its corporate and long-term strategy for granted without re-examination as circumstances change. What it can do is to adapt corporate planning and other management techniques by simplifying them; it might perhaps set up a part-time management services committee to introduce and control selected projects.

There is of course overlapping between the two categories mentioned here so that any distinction made may often seem to be one of convenience. It is however a very real one, which comes out clearly in the application of the computer, which for assignments of the first category is simply a means of getting through a lot of routine data processing and programmed decision-making quickly but which for the second category is to be seen as truly an aid to management policy-making and decision-making. The reason for this, ideally, should be that each company recognises its obligation to the community to produce the goods and services needed, without waste of any kind in so doing. There is also an implied obligation to maintain employment and to give employees a pride of accomplishment consistent with their talents. The social satisfaction of group co-operation inevitably follows industrial and commercial working and this too. contributes to effective working. On the economic plane every company is expected to make a contribution to the wellbeing of the community, so that better use is made of raw materials as they are converted into products, and of the indigenous labour force available for this conversion. To ease the national balance of payments problem exports are needed in greater volume, and these the most efficient companies are best able to contrive. Although some of these obligations may be imposed upon companies by legal restriction and Government controls, these measures are not sufficient in themselves to inculcate a striving for effectiveness throughout industrial and commercial working.

There is, however, a motivating factor that is perhaps even more potent in the search for effectiveness. This is the more personal aim of increasing the wealth or power of the company of individuals. There may be an ambition in the minds of directors to attain a dominant position in their industry; there may be a need to combat competition, particularly if alterations in tariff barriers have removed artificial restraints to international competition; there may be a requirement from owners that the profits available for distribution are increased year by year.

Any or all of these reasons may be the spur to encourage the search for greater effectiveness. This can be further personified by the practice of offering incentives to individuals to provide an artificial stimulant to their effectiveness of working. The chief executive may be paid by way of a salary plus a proportion of pre-tax profits, so that he is given a personal reason for exploiting to the full the means available to him to raise the level of profits earned.

Process research

The application of research and development work by the employment of scientists and technologist to discover better methods of working is a means of improving effectiveness that brings far-reaching long-term results. It is also the most direct way of introducing the methods of science to aid the operating management of a company. When process research is undertaken, a critical appraisal of the current methods of working is made to discover any inefficiencies that need to be corrected, and the reasons for them. The project to which the attention of the research worker is directed may present itself on grounds of time, cost or difficulty, but, once the project is decided upon, the application of scientific laws allows the evolution of a theory that can be tested by experiment under laboratory conditions and, if necessary, on a pilot plant of scale proportions.

As an example of this type of research, the time taken to harden-off a films of cellulose applied to a metal surface may preclude the use of an automatic flow of production throughout the factory. To improve the efficiency of working, some method of rapid hardening-off is required. Research would therefore be undertaken in the laboratory to discover such a method. The problem would be stuaied in theory, from the composition of the cellulose to the present method of application, to find the objective of the operation. If this is found to be the removal of the solvents used to float the solids evenly over the surface being coated, it is resolved into a drying problem. Experimental work would then be undertaken on methods of drying by various forms of the application of heat. Whether heat is applied by radiation or convection the result may be found to be equally undesirable—the outer skin hardening-off to leave behind a soft sandwich of semi-liquid cellulose between the metal and the skin. This would quickly "bleed" if the top skin were bruised and punctured, and an unsightly blemish would mar the surface finish. The application of heat from the inside of the cellulose film would appear to be what is required, but this would involve heating the metal surface which the cellulose is covering. This might to be too cumbersome a proposition in view of the large surface area of the product. It would also be impracticable when considered in relation to different sections of material that make up the fabricated part having to be heated, with consequent distortion on cooling. The answer to the problem might eventually be found to be the use of infra-red heacters. These operate with no radiation onto the surface of the cellulose film which would harden the surface first. By the use of this method, the film could be hardened-off from the inside out, so that the entire thickness of cellulose would be hard enough to withstand the rigours of the atmosphere to which it will be subjected in sue. Even though the solution is now in sight, the method of application has still to be determined. Further research by theory and experimentation is necessary to find the best way of subjecting the work to the action of the heater. After various trials, culminating in the prototype construction of the equipment and testing its use on actual products, the method finally evolved might be to pass the part by conveyor through a "tunnel" along which it is subjected to the action of many heaters surrounding it. The length of the tunnel, coupled with speed of the conveyor, would allow an adequate time for the hardening-off to be completed by the time the part emerges. By placing the tunnel on the line of production at the appropriate position, the work would flow through processing without interruption and a contribution would have been made by research to the greater effectiveness with which the work can be accomplished.

By scientific methods of research and investigation fundamental changes in processing methods have taken place in all industries. In metal working, the separate machine tools necessary for converting materials to the form and dimension required have been combined in the development of machines that perform a number of operations at a single work-station. By integrating a method of handling with the machining process, transfer machines have been developed for the completion of a multiplicity of different types of operation by one machine composed of a large number of work-heads. In steel working, improvements have followed from the introduction of a mixed oxygen/steam blast to the surface of the molten metal in the converter. The blast furnace operation of pig iron production has been improved by the injection of oil or alternatively coal dust, to supplement the coke content of the burden charged in. In textile working, inventions like the full width temple for use on the loom have reduced warp breakages and eliminated the damaged cloth associated with the use of conventional temples.

Work study

In British Standard 3138, *A Glossary of Terms Used in Work study,* there is a definition of the two techniques, Method Study and Work Measurement which in combination make up what is now widely known as work study. It is as follows:

(a) Method study is the systematic recording and analysis of existing methods of doing work and comparison with proposed new methods, together with the assessment of easier and more effective methods;

(b) Work measurement is the application of techniques designed to establish the time for a qualified worker to carry out a specified job at a defined level of performance.

Although work study does not require highly trained scientists or technologists it is as much a discipline as mechanical, electrical and civil engineering or chemistry and physics. It is true also, however, that there are very many people who can be taught quite quickly the systematic procedure of which it makes use. It is based on three assumptions:

(1) That there is usually "one best way" in which to carry out a task, Numerous ways will usually exist and be practised, but the knowledge available at any one time points to one method as better than the others. However, if some of the basic factors are changed, further improvements may well become possible.

(2) That a scientific method of solving problems is more productive of better work methods than is undisciplined ingenuity. This scientific method can be summarised as: the systematic observation of what actually happens, the search for an explanation which fit the facts and the finding of a hypothesis which seems to account for everything, and establishing whether the hypothesis is the correct one, something which in work study is done largely by experiment.

(3) That an allowed time for a task or a standard of performance may be determined so as to permit the most effective organisation and control of human activity.

In introducing *method study*, which is sometimes known as methods improvement or methods design, the scientific method requires that a systematic procedure be applied. The objects may include the improvement of processes and procedures, of factory, shop and workplace layout and the design of plant and equipment, the economy of human effort and the reduction of fatigue, the improved use of materials, machines and manpower, and the development of a better physical working environment.

The right attitude of mind is essential. This means, among other things, a desire and a determination to produce results, the ability to do so, and an understanding of the human factors involved.

Let us begin by stressing the fact that good human relations, with full and frank consultation at all levels, is an absolute pre-requisite of a successful method study project. There must be a clear definition of its purpose and some education of all levels of management and supervision in the use of work study techniques. Nor is this any less true of work measurement than of method study.

Persuading people to change their habit patterns is never easy but is made even more difficult in applying the results of method study; they may seem to imply adverse criticism.If a person without knowledge of the job can devise a better method of working relatively quickly, some criticism may be inferred of supervisors and operatives who are highly skilled at the job and yet have been adhering to the less effective method for many years. The investigator will need skill in handling people if he is to over-come this problem; this is part of a study which provides excellent training for management and is one of the reasons for the policy adopted in some companies of giving all management trainees a period on work study projects.

To return to the systematic procedures of method study. They can be summarised as follows:

(1) *Selecting and defining the job or process* to be studied. Efforts should be directed to solve those problems which are likely to yield the maximum return for the work done. Also, a general statement of the objective should be made.

It is probably advisable at the outset to define the problem in its broadest terms. This will allow greater freedom for the use of imagination and ingenuity. Nevertheless, one must not shirk the full diagnosis and clear statement of the problem. To do so may itself establish the basic cause.

One important point is to select the criteria by which one is to judge the successful solution of the problem. To determine the measure of success means that what is to be achieved must be known, e.g. the expenditure of less labour time, better usage of equipment, fewer operations, economies of space and fewer workers on the job.

(2) *Recording* from direct observation everything that happens. A variety of recording techniques exist; the choice between them depends

on the type and extent of the detail required. Analytical techniques such as process charts, multiple activity charts and activity sampling enable detailed studies to be made of the way in which work is done.

A feature common to most of these recording techniques is the use of diagrams and annotated symbols in order to avoid lengthy verbal descriptions. Alternatively, film studies may be used, giving the facilities of slow-motion re-running of film "takes" or conversely speeding up the running of the "take". Time lapse photography has one exposure taken every few seconds in a slow-moving job, with the speeding up of the process when the film is projected.

(3) *Examining the recorded facts critically* and challenging everything which is done, to determine the true reason underlying each event, the purpose of the activity, the place where it is performed, the sequence in which it is done, the person doing it and the means employed.

(4) *Developing the best method.* This is the search for possible solutions by applying the principles of motion economy, by using a process of elimination, by looking at the design of the product, by creative imagination and by advice from other specialists. One must determine the method which will best satisfy the criteria already adopted.

There will have to be a presentation, written and/or oral of the work study man's report, with supporting data. He often has a very real task of selling the new method and must anticipate possible objections and be prepared with answers to questions asked.

When the best method has been determined and agreed, it must be standardised. A written standard practice giving a detailed record of the operation and specifications for performing the work is the most common method of preserving the standard.

A carefully developed method is of no value unless an operator is available to work in the prescribed manner; therefore systematic training is often needed, including the re-training of experienced operators.

(5) The agreed method can then be *installed* as standard practice.

(6) *Maintaining and reviewing* the new method. It will be necessary to review the new procedures to maintain the benefits originally obtained. It may be that the criteria with which one started will in due course cease to be valid. Management decisions may alter requirements, employee suggestion schemes may throw up still further improvements; innovations may be introduced by supervisors or operatives. There should be a procedure for maintaining and reviewing a method of work.

So much for the technique of method study, but what of the complementary *work measurement*? This also is applied systematically but there is nothing like the unanimity about its application that there is about the method study stages stated above. Job knowledge and skill in assessment of human activity are required by the work measurement investigator.

Let us first of all quote a definition of work measurement from BSI 10003P "The application of techniques designed to establish the time for a qualified worker to carry out a specific job at a defined level of performance". In practice, the most satisfactory results are obtained when the most suitable techniques from the fields of method study and work measurement are applied to problems as complementary activities.

In many forms of industrial and commercial activity, standards of performance accepted as adequate may be lower than they need to be. Work measurement, if properly used, can determine a standard of performance within the reach of all qualified, properly trained and experienced operatives for a particular job.

Other aims may include more efficient manning of plant, improved planning and control, a basis for a sound incentive scheme, reliable performance indices and efficient labour cost control. With the rise in relative importance of indirect factory labour there has been a marked increase in office work. Some companies have brought these within the scope of their work study department but today there is more specialisation and although the philosophy of work study remains applicable, this particular branch of study is known as Organisation and Methods (O. & M.).

Work measurement is understandably very much concerned with the setting of time standards for tasks and a number of technique have been evolved. They include:

(a) *Time study,* which is carried out by performing one or more of the following techniques: stop-watch, cine-camers, moving tape machine record, electronic timber or tape recorder;

(b) *Use of elemental data.* In this type of technique, synthetic times or synthesised time standards for a job are built up from element times previously obtained from direct time studies of existing jobs. They are sometimes known as basic data or standard date;

(c) Predetermined Motion Time Systems, known as PMTS;

(d) Analytical estimating, used where no two jobs are identical and even where the same job is repeated on more than one occasion it will turn out to have varied times of performance:

(e) *Work sampling.* Sometimes the work of a section may be so widely varied that a time study or element breakdown and synthetic times are not applicable. A picture of the activity can be obtained by taking a series of studies at different times and according to a set sampling pattern. The pattern of the work can then be determined from these random observations.

A number of features are common to all forms of work measurement whatever the technique applied to a specific study. They include:

(a) An identification of distinct *elements of work*. Elements of motion are the movements which recur whenever the task being observed is repeated. If we divide the complete work cycle of a job into elements we can study in detail the duration of each element.

(b) The recognition of variations in the methods and skills of the worker.

(c) *The practice of rating*. This means setting a typical or representative method and then measuring according to a rating scale the deviations in speed and effectiveness from this standard rating.

The practice of rating rests on a concept of a standard performance and this is defined in BS 3138 as "a rate of output which qualified workers will naturally achieve without over-exertion as an average over the working day or shift, provided they know and adhere to the specified method and provided they are motivated to apply themselves to their work".

The most widely used system makes use of a scale which is based on an assumption that non-meentive performance represents 60 minutes' worth of work in the hour. This performance is given a figure of 60, which is called the rating factor. Incentive performance, being one-third faster than non-incentive performance, represents 80 minutes' worth of work in the hour and its rating factor is 80. The system is known as the 60/80 Rating Scale.

There are of course other scales, notably the 100/133 Rating Scale and a British Standard 0/100 Scale.

(d) The concept of a *basic time* required to perform the operation by an operative who is applying his skill, effort and concentration at the standard rating.

(e) *Allowances.* A worker needs time for relaxation and personal needs, in preparation for production, dealing with contingencies, and process delay during which he is perforce idle. An allowance of time to meet these needs must therefore be added to the basic standard time, being expressed as a standard of that time. The simplest method is to apply a flat percentage to the total cycle time but where conditions are variable a more systematic approach may be required.

Finally, may one look briefly at Methods Time Measurement (MTM) and MTM 2, probably the best known of the predetermined motion time systems? MTM was introduced into the U.S.A. in the late 1940s and spread widely there although it never obtained so strong a hold in Britain or the rest of Europe, with some exceptions such as Sweden. It is most useful when applied to short cycle work where thousands and perhaps millions of parts, have to be handled, tested and assembled. It rests on an assumption that any manual job is made up of a number of basic motions or factors. These basic motions (known as elements) can be combined in an almost infinite number of sequences according to the nature of the job. They are:

Reach;	Release;
Move;	Disengage;
Turn and Apply Pressure;	Eye Travel Time and Eye Focus;
Grasp;	Body, Leg and Foot Motions.
Position:	

Any one of these motions can be sub-divided. There are thus 18 sub-classifications of "Position". However, provided the time for carrying out each basic motion can be established, it is possible to work out a set of standard times needed for the performance of a wide variety of manual jobs without having to make a direct time study.

When a task has been selected for analysis the first main step is to record it in terms of elements of motion. The correct identification of elements is an all-important preliminary. When the manual operation has been analysed into the basic motions required to perform it, the next step is to assign to each motion a pre-determined time standard governed by the nature of the motion and the conditions under which it is made. In the MTM system, such times are expressed in TMU's, i.e. in time measurement units. All the motions involved are accounted for, and by this method the controversial rating factor used in stop-watch studies is eliminated. Normal allowances for fatigue, unavoidable delays and other such factors are added to the standard time obtained.

MTM 2 is a more recent simplification of the original MTM. Motions have been combined to yield a smaller number of categories and the effect of this and certain other changes is to make the system much faster in operation; it is claimed that only one-quarter of the time needed for MTM is required in the application of MTM 2.

Management audit

Both process research and works study are narrowly concentrated on matters of operating effectiveness, but in many companies it may be more important to consider the broader context within which the operations occur. Instead of considering a process or operation in isolation, in order to concentrate attention upon its effectiveness, management activities. Which make the processes possible, are considered in detail. From this, a greater overall effect may result. The word "audit" has come to be associated with accounts and to be thought of as meaning an examination and verification of records. The same word has been applied to the examination and verification of the management structure and the practices and procedures by which managers carry out their work in an undertaking. This is a further application of the scientific management philosophy of dissatisfaction with present affairs and the constant striving for their betterment.

A comprehensive management audit of a particular business will have as its objective the determination of the present position of the business by assessment of the results of its operations in relation to recognised standards. The aim is to reveal imperfection of any type and to make suggestions for their correction. This involves consideration of the capital structure of the business, the organisation structure and the policies and practices of management. The external aspects of markets served and sources of material utilised are also considered. Despite the importance of the position of any company in its general environment, the chief direction of examination is inwards, particularly towards the co-ordination of the working of the various divisions of the enterprise.

It is possible, of course, to restrict the examination to something less than such a comprehensive survey so that, for example, any trends towards unusual or ineffective practices can be exposed, or the affairs of a particular division of the company can be investigated. By such methods of checking, it is possible to provide the managers with a periodic assurance of the effectiveness of operations of the enterprise. It may be thought that this is already being given by the annual profit and loss account figures, but this is not so. No accountancy records provide a complete picture of the efficiency of a company, particularly when they are considered in isolation.

So many of the features of ineffectiveness are insidious in their effect, and take a long time to make their presence felt in statements of account, that it is desirable to expose them as early as possible, so that the unusual trend can be corrected before its effect is accentuated.

The starting point for a comprehensive audit is obviously the organisation structure. The intention is to check its appropriateness for its purpose. Although some consideration has to be paid to the personalities employed and the traditions built up in the company over the years, the fundamental design should be sufficiently impersonal and flexible to copy with anticipated changes. The audit usually reveals a tendency for the structure to be out of balance for its present purpose as a result of hap-hazard growth, a condition especially associated with the growing power of certain executives who have engaged in their own efforts at "empire" building. An independent check exposes this and enables suggestions to be made for corrective action.

Apart from organisation, but contributory to its effective employment in practice, are the techniques and procedures used by the company. It may be that no plan has been made for any investigations of process research or work study type; there may be no present concern for the elements of planning and control to be separated from operations; an inadequate provision of specialist aid for line management may be apparent in the structure. The exposure of any such deficiencies leads to the specification of appropriate action, in the light of the company's needs.

A management audit is essentially unique to a particular enterprise. The results cannot be more widely applied. There is, however, in all audits a common feature of investigation and check for which it is possible to lay down a series of queries to be posed in relation to the detailed working of the organisation. It is therefore preferable for an external investigator skilled in the examination procedure to be engaged by the company to undertaken the audit. This then becomes consultancy, in which certain highly qualified groups specialise. In the popular press, the consultant is often referred to as a company doctor. There is some truth in this analogy since it suggests an examination of the body of the company to diagnose the reasons for a lack of expected performance and the prescription of the cure to be taken. The analogy falls down in the initial identification of the ailment, since the patient has feelings and can state the symptoms, whereas the company has no feelings, is inarticulate, and unlike the body is not necessarily a composite whole whose co-ordinated working can be seen. It is therefore necessary for audits to be undertaken periodically, to ensure that the growth and changes taking place are accompanied by changes to maintain effectiveness of working. The suggested period for a review of the co-ordinated affairs of the whole company is of the order of five years.

Inter-firm comparison.

In determining the present position of a business, in overall terms as in detailed working, it is an advantage to have known standards for comparison. This is not a request for idealistic standards, but for some idea to be available of the practical accomplishments of other companies of similar type and size. The relative efficiency of the firm can then be determined. To permit such comparison it is necessary for each company to be prepared to submit figures of its results to a clearing house. To preserve secrecy, these can be hidden under a cloak of anonymity. Some trade associations and central management institutions such as the British Institute of Management run schemes for inter-firm comparison. Through taking part in a series of inter-firm statistical comparisons it is possible for a company to obtain information of use in testing its own effectiveness of working.

Planning and control techniques reveal ineffectiveness and spotlight the need for corrective action, but these are purely internal to the company. They do not provide any guide to the real efficiency of the company. Even with their use, and the consequent establishment of better performance, there is no certainty that other comparable businesses have not achieved even higher levels of effectiveness. A case therefore can be made for participation in a scheme which makes available a wider range of comparative data than can be derived from within the company's own resources. The basic principle for effective comparison is that the statistics used should be truly comparable. This may mean that the results of operations in particular firms have to be adjusted before being contributed to the scheme. Since the ultimate objective of inter-firm comparison is to find reasons for variances in the figures submitted by different firms, the figures must not be adjusted too freely or the benefit of comparison will be lost. A simple comparison can be made on unit cost of manufacture, but for this to be possible it is necessary to eliminate the fixed element from production costs, since administrative costs vary so widely from firm to firm. The comparison of these fixed costs can then be made later by means, for example, of the ratio of fixed overheads to capital employed. For unit cost to be truly comparable, throughput must be expressed in a common unit that forms the basis of comparison for all participants in the scheme. It is also necessary to take into account the different methods of production used, so that the costs of the unit of input and output are related to specific types of plant or methods of production.

Ratios, rather than definite figures of units of output or costs incurred are widely used for comparison. For example, the return on capital is a useful figure since it gives an overall rating of the effectiveness of business. The difficulty of comparison is to ensure that all firms participating in the scheme calculate their returns and their capital in the same way.The returns may be deemed to be the operating profit from the activities of the company. All firms must interpret it in the same way. When calculating capital it is not necessary to consider how the capital has been contributed. All that is of concern is the amount available, so that the efficiency of the firm can be judged by the return on capital employed. Again, it is essential for all concerns to include the same type of capital if the comparison is to be effective. It may be decided that the capital shall be deemed to comprise total assets, excluding cash holding and outside investments, but the problem then arising is the valuation of assets. Are these to be included at original cost, book value or current replacement costs? Another important factor may be the size of building used. It may therefore be decided to exclude the value of the premises from the reckoning of capital but instead to reduce operating profit by a charge for rent. From these examples, it is seen that the determination of a fair comparison is not a simple matter. Significant ratios must be selected and the rules for their calculation must be laid down so that all firms compute their figures in the same way.

Each participant in the scheme receives a report of information composed of either a list of all the figures submitted or an average figure, with the range indicated. This permits each firm to determine exactly where it stands relative to all the others, in regard to every comparison listed. The problem then posed for the firm with an unfavorable comparison is: why are other companies able to achieve higher efficiency, or lower cost? This concentrates attention on the apparent causes of weakness. Investigations can then be made by managers to find a solution which will lead to increased efficiency of the company.

Cost reduction

Inter-firm comparison data often provides the impetus for the introduction of cost reduction programmes. One of the indications of lack of effectiveness is a high cost factor at some point in the company's operations. Discovery of this fact would lead to an attempt to reduce cost to bring the concern into line with others in the industry. But it is not only through inter-firm comparison that cost reduction will be sought. Every firm should adopt a philosophy of minimum cost in its everyday affairs. Although the technical aspects of utilisation of materials, plant and manpower are involved, cost reduction is usually achieved by a careful consideration of the procedures adopted, so that they all contribute to general effectiveness of operations.

In the large company an office section concerned with employing all possible techniques for the continuous reduction of operating costs may be justified. This is not the same as cost control, which is concerned only with the setting of standards with which the actual cost can be compared, nor is it to be likened to budgetary control, with its restriction of expenditure in every detailed centre. Cost reduction is a positive search for more effective operations as a result of which operating costs will be minimised. If a company is not large enough to support a separate department of engineers and accountants with specific responsibilities for cost reduction, it may still benefit by inculcating in all managers the idea that cost matters. If all waste is avoided and supervisors are periodically trained in cost reduction programmes, so that they can more critically consider their own jobs, and those of their subordinates, improved effectiveness of operations will follow. As overall operating cost is reduced by positive action, rather than by holding down the level of expenditure artificially, an increased margin, revealed by the accounts, should be a true reflection of improvement. Cost reduction can be aimed at in every company, no matter what its size or type of product may be. It is a positive way of striving for increased effectiveness.

Higher control

The higher control method attributed to T.G. Rose was quoted as an example of a method by which the trend of company affairs can be followed at top level by the submission of monthly reports. It is now appropriate to consider such a method since, by its use, the effectiveness of the management of a business can be assessed and attention directed to any changes what will have a beneficial effect in the future.

The system of higher control is a valuable one as it applies broadly to all types and sizes of company. It is simple, yet accurate in results. The underlying idea is to process existing company records to facilitate their use, rather than to super-impose extra controls. Although concerned with an expression of the position of the company in financial terms, control is not simply a rehash of accounts information; it is a thoroughly planned approach to the presentation of useful figures to top management. In addition to the existing cost and financial information, there are some extra reports that particular executives are required to submit, which perhaps they would not do normally, but this is beneficial to them in their own work, as it focuses their attention on the essential of their job by the very act of having to submit comments on events to the managing director at least once a month.A monthly rendering of accounts is necessary instead of relying solely on the annual statements, but the control reports which include this data are submitted later than those containing non-financial information. Thus, time is allowed in the system for the extra work involved.

In keeping with the general approach to control techniques in scientific management, the system of higher control relies upon a factual basis for the monthly report submitted to the managing director. The activities of the company are surveyed each month from different aspects by the comparison of trends. The results of any one period are not then considered in isolation but by means of a comparison with those of the immediately preceding twelve-month period. All the statistics used for a comparison of trends are illustrated by line diagrams, which are largely self-explanatory indicators of success. This is achieved by charting correlated items in such a way that an upward tendency of the line indicates improvement, downward indicates the reverse. This is true even for the ratios used to indicate changes in the financial position. They are so constructed that improvements are shown by a rise in their numerical value. The scheme lays down a routine of reporting upon the main facts necessary for the exercise of effective control. The business position can be watched through such items as the order book position. As the size of the order book establishes the activity of the business for some period ahead, any fluctuation of orders provides a prior indication of the company's future business position. Both the sales manager and the works manager can contribute useful reports on orders received and outstanding, to provide a clear picture of the business position. The company's financial books show the effectiveness of this handling of company affairs in relation to external trading and the internal financial position. It is necessary for this purpose to prepare a profit and loss account each month so that the trading position can be viewed. For details of the financial position, a balance sheet has to be prepared and from it certain ratios can be used to show the current position. All these reports, together with those on the technical position in research all manufacture, are submitted to the managing director. From them he compiles his own report to the board. Higher control thus provides a means of checking the results following the implementation of policies formulated by the board. The value of the system lies in the prompt submission of interpreted information about company affairs, so that any unfavourable trends can be detected in sufficient time for corrective action to be taken. A contribution is thus made to the continued effectiveness of the enterprise.

Automation

The provision of information that arises from a comparison of expectation and achievement shows whether the progress of affairs accords with the plans laid down. The reporting of information on unfavourable comparisons permits remedial action to be specified and applied so that there is the minimum reduction of operating effectiveness. The usual systems for the provision of control information associated with the practical application of scientific management techniques have been referred to as *open loop systems.* This means that information has to be fed out from the process in order that the necessary comparisons can be made. It is only a short step along the road of increased mechanisation to close the loop so that the intervention of a person is not required to complete the control circuit. Operating systems can then be made self-correcting to produce the desired performance. Automatic machinery has been used for a long time since, for example, Jacquard's "programming" of the loom by punched cards early in the nineteenth century, and the early twentieth-century "automatics" which were used in metal-cutting operations. The machinery to which the term automatic has been applied in the past is merely self-operating. It incorporates a "memory" unit to provide the initiative for the sequence of activities to be undertaken. This it will repeat as long as material is supplied and power is available. The repetitive acts will proceed whether they are right or wrong; the machine is not sensible of its own results. A more sophisticated machine is given a sensibility to its own activities which amounts, by analogy, to a conscience in that it can determine right from wrong. There is also an inbuilt facility for correction, so that deviations are kept within defined limits.

This further step along the path of mechanisation was first described as "automaticisation", but this cumbersome word has been contracted to *automation*. This refers to the use of mechanisms to operate factory equipment. The immediate management implications are evident. Since operatives are not needed for direct work on such equipment, fewer workers are employed in automatic factories and fewer human problems arise in day-by-day management. A secondary feature is the absence of the need for control data on which action can be taken to keep operations in step with requirements, since this is largely taken care of within the machine systems. The general emphasis of management then tends towards a high degree of technical competence in the jobs being performed by the machines, and in the appreciation of the character of the automatic procedures being used. This gives rise to the need for longer periods of training for managers, in technology rather than in human relations, although the latter are still important.

From the outset of operations, it is necessary to achieve a greater integration of processes with a resulting increase in the complexity of manufacturing activity. Automatic control should be widespread in application if full advantage is to be gained from its use. To apply it piecemeal, to separate operations or processes, usually exposes the inadequacy of the intermediate activities, which cannot generally be operated with the same efficiency nor at the same tempo as the automated operations. Greater attention must therefore be paid to planning and to the design of machines and processes to ensure that the optimum effectiveness is derived from a thorough integration. Emphasis is thus removed from the physical aspects of manufacture to the provisions made to make it possible. This inevitably increases the ratio of clerical workers to workers in the more practical occupations of the factory. A startling effect of the introduction of automatic control to an integrated system of processing is the need for extensive capital investment. The necessary technical equipment is complex and costly when applied to an entire factory but this effect can be minimised by the use of low-cost automated devices such as are achieved by attaching control mechanisms to existing machinery. When this course is pursued, it must be recognised as second best, since it is not possible to gain the full advantages of a more fundamental approach merely by introducing innovations to existing processing methods as a result of applied research.

If a large investment has been made in tooling-up the factory, there must be the expectation of a high degree of utilisation of machines on productive work. This has two effects:

The operation of the machinery for the maximum possible time during any period; and

The concentration of control information on setting times and standing times, instead of on operating data.

The first of these effects introduces the need for shift working where this is not already the practice. The optimum expected in practice is often sixteen hours a day on direct operations, with the reminder of the day spent on maintenance and remedial work. If the character of the work is such that an operation on once started must be completed without interruption, this will involve round-the-clock working—but this is not a problem unique to automated factories. The effect of the change of character of control information, when considered in conjunction with the reduced number of workers for whom each manager is responsible, changes the character of the management task to a concentration on "trouble shooting". The manager then becomes a specialist in remedial work, the specification of which is accurately determined by the diagnostic control information available to him.

The greater extremes of worker skills required in the automated factory pose problems for management. The larger proportion of workers in office occupations brings in its train some need for critical appraisal of the clerical procedures in use, to ensure that the greater effectiveness of technical operations is not being offset by an increase in undesirable paperwork procedures. On the factory floor, the machine operator's task is usually upgraded to the setting of the machinery and control mechanisms to prepare them for the specific use to which they are put, and to the carrying out any remedial work necessary on the machine when the ability of the mechanisms for self-correction is exhausted. The upgrading of the skills of many workers intensifies the problems of initial selection, continued training and constant motivation. New trades are introduced into the operating situation for maintenance of the complex hydraulic, or electronic sensing mechanisms used on machinery, thus introducing a broader range of technical matters of which the operating manager must have a sound appreciation.

When the low-cost automation is applied, or in circumstances where manpower has still to be used for machine operation, the psychological problems of machine pacing of work introduce an additional factor to be handled by the manager. The increased dependence on speeds of machine working generally makes the use of financial incentives impossible. Job evaluated wages structures then assume greater importance but do not, in themselves, remove the manual worker's irritation at the machine which is governing his behaviour.

It has been suggested that planners and machine designers, as well as operating managers, are involved in changes on the adoption of systems of automatic control. Another specialist manager whose work is radically altered is the accountant. The financial implications of investment and utilisation sufficient to achieve a fair return on capital have been referred to, but the more radical changes accompanying automated methods of production are clearly reflected in cost data. For costing purposes it is usual to distinguish between direct and indirect labour. No such distinction can be made in the automatic factory; all labour is indirect in type. This is particularly emphasised by the much larger proportion of maintenance costs incurred. New criteria are therefore needed for cost systems and elements of a fundamentally different character are required as the basic building blocks from which the cost data relating to operations is compiled.

It will therefore be seen that there are many ways in which a manager's practices change on the introduction of automatic control systems.

Applications are generally restricted to industries that lend themselves to flow-line production of a small range of standardised parts. Repetition of routine activities is the key feature demanded of any process sequence to be subjected to automatic methods of control.

The biggest management problem arising from the introduction of automated methods of working has been the much smaller labour force required for their continued working, compared with the systems replace. It has not been uncommon for hundreds of workers to become redundant on the introduction of new equipment. This is an effect of progress, but it cannot be shrugged off. All companies have a social obligation towards "their employees. A loyal worker should not be discharged casually because a machine can do his work more effectively. Redeployment of the labour force must be carried out and natural wastage can be used to run down the total number of workers. A clearly defined redundancy procedure is an essential outcome of the employment policy of every company.

Computers in the factory

Automatic methods of control may require the use of rapid methods of calculation to determine the programme of work to be carried out by a machinery or equipment. In the numerical control of the machine tools that are the basic machines used in metal-working industries, the machine is given instructions in the form of numbers for the motion of slides and cutting heads. The instructions cause servo-mechanisms, slave motors which respond to the orders of a master, to position the machine parts precisely at every stage of operation. The motions of the machinery are initiated by the introduction to the machine operation cabinet of numerical positioning information which has been coded onto punched paper or card by a computer. By the use of computer information to guide the machine, more complicated parts can be produced with greater speed and accuracy at lower cost.

This example of machine control by computer has been introduced at the outset to indicate an application of computer information to process control. This form of application is perhaps of greatest significance to the ultimate effectiveness of production. Many more complex systems of process control by computer are available; in these the condition of plant and equipment is constantly checked by a monitoring system. The sensing of size, temperature, pressure, switch positions and many other types of control information can be carried out automatically and speedily by using a computer. Process monitoring is carried out by sensing operating data and checking this against predetermined values. Action is taken when a change from normal to abnormal is detected. The basic principle is therefore the same as that used in the less sophisticated manual systems considered earlier, including the principle of exceptions. By using a computer, it is not only possible to sense the condition at many hundreds of points continuously but also to store data within the computer so that it can make comparisons between expectation and achievement.

When the operations for which control is required extend over a wide range of processing conditions, it may be necessary to employ a number of computers in the same factory, each of which is purpose-made for a section of the work. In the steel works, for example, a control hierarchy may need to be built up to cover all processes from restocking to dispatch of the cut, rolled section. The calculation of the steel to be produced to meet customer requirements can be speedily completed and fed to another computer for breaking down the production schedule into operating details for points throughout the manufacturing sequence. The plant control computer transmits instructions to the various sections of the plant and receives by return the operating details that have been automatically sensed at various points in processing. Any production changes received are incorporated in modifications to the original instructions fed to later stages of processing, so that a decision-making process is carried out continuously in the computer to keep the flow of production in balance.

Although it may appear that computers are far-seeing, rapid-acting geniuses when used for automatic control of processing there are many limitations to their use which must be recognised by managers who take advantage of them. The computer can be given a memory, it can also be programmed to act sensibly, *but it has no experience outside that information by which to form a judgment* to cope with unusual occurrences. The manager is not outside by the computer, which is not intended for use in place of human managers-although it may well replace lower-grade clerical workers. Decision making is still necessary even when the computer is employed. The principal advantage arising from its use is the instantaneous availability of operating data so that every other point in processing affected by it can be speedily informed and given revised instructions immediately. Each section or department is given information about what has happened at every other stage of the manufacturing cycle.

In addition to its use for direct plant control, the computer can be used to provide an advanced technique of planning and control in the type of factory where the jobs undertaken are so diverse that a fully integrated scheme of manufacture is not possible. By the use of a computer for data processing it is possible to provide greater assurance of continuous high rates of output without costly delays. *It is emphasised that the computer is clerical aid for rapid provision of information; it does not make the manager's decisions for him.* For use on planning and control work, the computer usually has a large input of data on which relatively few mathematical operations have to be performed. It is not so much a computer then, since calculations are a minor part of its work, but more correctly a comparator and information store. The vast amount of information needed for production control is indicated by the experience of one company which needed more than one and a quarter million separate items of data at some time during production planning and control. This was for a factory employing only 500 workers on the manufacture of a few hundred different products, comprising, in total, some two thousand distinct parts. The advantage gained from such an application is speed of processing data, coupled with the rapid availability of the processed information. In such a way the use of the computer ensures more effective control of production by ascertaining that all the factors of production are employed appropriately.

In would be expected that the use of the computer for data-processing is not confined to operations of direct effect on manufacture. Earlier references to the detailed procedures of scientific management should have created the impression of a great deal of random fact being collected and processed for a variety of purposes. The computer can be used for many of these purposes, with consequent improvement in the speed and accuracy of data processing.

Simulation

Simulation is a technique which proceeds by preparing a model so as the better to be able to forecast the progress of the technology involved. In management services it constructs and manipulates an imitation or model of a real system. The model is dynamic and therefore by simulation with data from real situations it may be used to forecast changes and the behaviour of the system under various conditions. The technique has been adapted to computer simulation of complex industrial situations as an aid to decision making and policy formation by management.

There is obviously a close relationship to operational research techniques, although simulation is not necessarily mathematical in its operations. It may use a physical or semi-physical model in contrast to the analytical ones of the O.R. scientist. As a technique it is iterative; if the situation which is simulated is at all complex, a computer has to be applied before the exercise can get far, the sheer volume of calculations demanding computerisation even if nothing else does.

The method known as system simulation is enlisted in problem analysis, more particularly in the analysis of potential problems. Indeed, a decision maker will instinctively resort to simple simulation even if he has never heard of the practice in relation to management technology. He will make rough sketches, adopt broad financial estimates and extended drawings and diagrams to represent the emergence of projected trends.

More formally, a model is prepared and is tested by making successive changes in the factors which operate on it until the optimum course of action is discovered.

One could quote many examples of application to major functions in industry. One is the problem of making the best possible use of a transport fleet operated by a distributive company for its products. Another is a programme for cost reduction. A third example is the model of a competitive market with a view to forecasting the market trends for a product one is selling.One interesting recent example at Cranfield Institute of Technology has been a model used to diagnose the effects of alternative policies pursued by the firms in an industry and their Industrial Training Board—the figures and percentage of levy on firms for training and grants to them will be varied and the probable effect studied.

Another interesting case is the operating of port unloading facilities. A logical model of the port can be constructed and embodied in a computer programme. One may start with an arbitrarily chosen set of conditions and a given number of shipping berths, then run the model again and again on the computer to test the effects of having different numbers of berths until the optimum number can be selected. By doing so one is discovering facts more cheaply than would be possible by going through the actual situation.

Systems simulation has a number of advantages. It provides a frame of reference within which a problem can be studied. It throws light on the gaps in information and by doing so will often suggest lines of action to remedy them. The model can be tested so as to show up deficiencies which would otherwise have gone unnoticed. In decision making one necessarily has to make abstraction from the actual situation. Simulation brings this problem of abstraction into the open. The use of symbolic language enables the problem-solver to handle concepts more readily. And, equally important, it provides a cheap method of tackling prediction.

There are limitations. Simulation can hardly expect to escape the dangers inherent in all abstractions from reality, especially that of overmuch simplification. There are limits beyond which symbolic presentation is not valid.

Operational research

Even where ample facts are available, the manager's difficulty in decision making may sometimes be caused by the complexity of the variables in the problem. The human mind can after all only cope with a limited number of variables at the same time, and the ideal solution to this kind of dilemma is for the thinking to be carried out in a series of steps by which a decision is ultimately reached. Yet this type of logical approach is not common, while time often presses to insistently on the manager as to forbid the delay which must be caused by working out an ideal situation.

Yet huge financial and material resources may be at stake, new products and revolutionary technology. The viable size of a company exploiting some products cannot be other than very large. It is not surprising that the application of science to management has grown apace and that operational research has become an accepted feature of management technology, a long way on from the elementary scientific method advocated by F. W. Taylor and F. B. Gilbreth and the rest of the early Scientific Management movement.

Operational research itself must be regarded as something more than a single management technique. It is potentially much more, being based on a conviction that one can usefully construct a model of a really complex business or at least a major division of that business, i.e. it is tending towards the integration of a number of activities which have hitherto been pursued separately. It is also increasingly concerned with the evolution of competitive strategies and with the choice of scientific research and development programmes. The use of the adjective operational does not imply that the application is restricted to manufacturing operations and processes. This type of research is relevant to various management activities. The technical and clerical aspects of factory planning processes are particularly amenable to the application of operational research. Aspects of human relationships are involved in such arrangements and are amenable to O.R. investigation. Outside the confines of factory work O.R. is equally applicable to government operations, to the armed services and to large service industries such as transport and insurance.

Operational research provides a scientific and quantitative basis for decision making and offers solutions to business problems by mathematical means. Its aim is to reduce the part played by subjective judgment in making such decisions.

It begins by identifying the significant factors in a problem. It then established the way in which these facts act on one another. They are measured so as to assess the importance of each. Many can be expressed as mathematical formulae.

5 Management Education: Purposes, Policies and Evaluation

Strictly speaking, 'things' such as training programmes and management development procedures do not have purposes in their own right. It is only people who have purposes. Similarly there are many reasons why people may which to conduct evaluations of these things. For example, they may be wishing to: document events, record student changes, identify points of institutional vitality, place the blame for trouble on others, aid administrative decision making, facilitate corrective action, increase understanding of teaching and learning processes, make a case fro greater resources, and so on. It is only in an indirect sense that evaluations may be seen to contain any purposes of their own since their since their designs may embody the purposes of their instigators.

Whereas the purposes of individuals may cover such a wide range of aims that it is not feasible to provide an adequate framework for analysis it is possible to talk in more general terms about the purposes of evaluation studies. This will therefore form a starting point to this chapter, and it is also suggested that it should form a starting point to any evaluative activity. There are several reasons for this. First, there is some logic to the idea of being clear about why one is jumping into an activity before one does it - and a great deal of what passes for evaluation fulfils little more than a ritualistic function, the end-of-course questionnaire is circulated at the end of the course simply because people expend it to be so. Second, although some would disagree with this point, it is likely that a confusion over the purposes of an evaluation study will make it less able to serve adequately any single one of those purposes. Third, one of the difficulties in effecting implementation of evaluation work is that many of those involved tend to be rather circumspect about their true interests and purposes. It is, therefore, likely that some concentration upon identifying the purposes of an evaluation may help to flush out some of the hidden agendas of those involved. Not that this will solve all the problems of the valuator; but it might provide a reasonable start.

Three general purposes of evaluation

Although, as we shall see later, the approaches and styles adopted by authors and practitioners towards evaluation are almost as varied as their proponents, there is quite a high degree of consistency about what they consider to be the primary aim underlying their evaluative activities. The three that will be discussed here are those of: *proving, improving* and *learning*. The former aims to demonstrate conclusively that something has happened as a result of training or developmental activities, and that this may also be linked to judgements about the value of the activity: whether the right thing was done, whether it was well done, whether it was worth the cost, and so on. The second aim, 'improving' implies an emphasis on trying to ensure that either the current, or future programmes and activities become better than they are at present. The third aim recognises that evaluation cannot with ease be divorced from the processes upon which it concentrates, and therefore that this slight problem might well be turned to advantage by regarding evaluation as an integral part of the learning and development process itself. These three general purposes are illustrated in Figure.

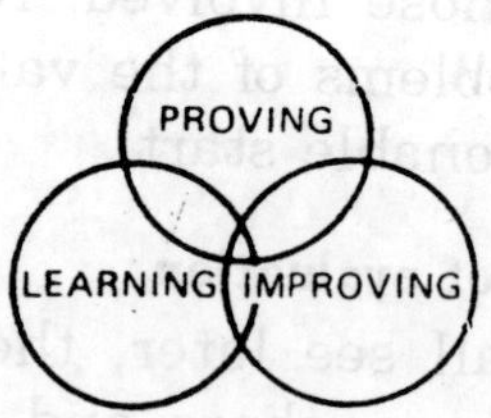

Figure : Three general purposes of evaluation

Three general purposes of evaluation

The emphasis on these three aims has changed

over the years, and in order they roughly parallel historical developments in evaluation thought during the 1960s, 1970s, and early 1980s. Inevitably, there are overlaps, and authors who have preferred one or other of these purposes have often acknowledged the existence of the other two. Moreover, there are also reasons why an evaluator may choose one particular aim over the others, beyond the dictates of fashion and methodological development, and as remarked in the first chapter, it would seem that economic pressures are placing an increasing onus upon the evaluator to prove the worth of training and other developmental activities. But before discussing the issue of choice it seems worth elaborating a little on the background to each of these general aims.

Proving

The emphasis on proving the worth and impact of training is where it all began. The first major evaluation study to be reported was that of the war-time Training Within Industry courses lasting ten hours through which over one million American supervisors received training. When asked by the House Appropriations' Committee for evidence that the expenditure on this programme was worthwhile, the TWI organisation was able to provide figures indicating that in two-thirds of the plants involved production increases of more than 25 per cent had been recorded since the training had taken place. Although it is probable that these production increases were caused by factors other than the supervisory training programme, this evidence was sufficiently impressive to maintain TWI in existence and it was even exported to Europe after the war as part of the attempt to reconstruct national industries. While the results in the TWI report provided adequate evidence according to the standards of the time, it is unlikely that this would be given much credence by modern researchers. Indeed, as standards of acceptability have risen, successful cost-benefit evaluations have been reported most infrequently. In the case of operative training there are a number of cases where evaluation studies have been able to make modest estimates of the financial benefits resulting from highly specified forms of training. But as Hamblin, points out, the problems become exceedingly difficult when considering the discretionary and non-programmable aspects of managerial work. Even in the present day there remain few convincing cost-benefit evaluations of management training, and opinion remains divided upon whether it is worth attempting. For example, a recent report to the Manpower Services Commission on the costing of training by Peat, Marwick, Mitchell and Company commented that although cost-benefit analysis might be appropriate for considering the economic and social effects of public investments in training and education on a 'grand' scale, 'the method does not seem appropriate for judging investments in training by an individual company'. Nevertheless, cost-benefit analysis of management training is still recommended by some authors, as the 'ultimate assessment'. Unfortunately, the example given by these authors is of a study which did not go beyond analysis of the *potential* cost-benefits of a programme, which was never run. To their credit they were able to demonstrate that the programme should *not* be run because the maximum potential benefits were likely to be far less than the costs of the programme. But the approach of cost-benefit analysis does not present the most optimistic future for evaluation.

Nevertheless, it is still argued by influential authorities such as Michael Scriven, that evaluators should always attempt to examine the *value* of any particular programme. According to Hesseling, 'evaluation research aims at providing a systematic and comprehensive measure of success or failure for training programmes. But, the problem remains that even it is possible to overcome the technical difficulties in measuring outcomes and changes resulting from managerial training and development, it has still to be decided against whose criteria of value such changes might be assessed. As Hopwood points out in an interesting discussion on the meaning of corporate effectiveness, notions of what are good and desirable behaviours for managers are not universal. They may be presented as if they are self-evident and objectively determined, but in fact they are often articulated primarily to serve the interests and demands of powerful groups within organisations, 'and as such interests and contexts vary and change over time, so do the prevailing notions of effectiveness, so also, it is with notions of the value of procedures intended to change managerial behaviour.

Before leaving this discussion about the problem, of proving the effects of management training it is worth noting two possible ways of resolving the problem of having multiple criteria of value. First, those involved in evaluation might identify the most influential stakeholders in relation to the programme and simply attempt to present evaluative information within the framework of value held by each individual. Second, one might take a more catholic approach by identifying all the main stakeholders involved with the programme, and attempting to identify what criteria they would use in assessing the value of the programme. Peter Critton recommends this approach in relation to clients, learners,designer/change agents, and the organisation. Any evaluative information can then be collected with these multiple criteria in mind.

Improving

Michael Scriven's emphasis upon assessing the *value* of a programme, was formulated in contrast to an earlier view of Cronbach that 'greatest service evaluation can perform is to identify aspects of the course where revision is desirable'. This he labelled as *formative* evaluation which is aimed at *improving* whatever product is under investigation. Writers on the evaluation of management training have tended to stress this particular purpose, partly as a reaction to the difficulties of *proving* anything about the effects of training. Thus, Warr, Bird and Rackham state that; 'the primary purpose of gathering evaluation and data is to provide the trainer with information which will help him increase his subsequent effectiveness. And Hamblin after some hopeful comments earlier in the book about the analysis of potential benefits, commitments that the purpose of evaluation'is not to determine if desired changes did occur but rather to *determine what should happen next*.... There is vast support for improving as a valid purpose to evaluation, although one suspects that but for technical difficulties many authors would have preferred this to have been a purpose subsidiary to proving.

Learning

The possibility that evaluation may contributor directly to the *learning* process has received less attention in the literature than either of the above two purposes, But there are still one or two examples. Warr, Bird, and Rackkam provide evidence of a pre-course questionnaire, administered as part of an evaluation study, having a positive impact on the learning of supervisions attending an accident prevention course. This example may be regarded as an instance of the well-known Hawthorne effect at work: where the attempt to observe something actually changes the thing that one is observing. Alternatively this may be used to advantages as part of the training process: the knowledge that one's success at learning is likely to be assessed at the end of the days tends to concentrate the mind wonderfully.

This may be seen by some as rather manipulative, and Hesseling suggests that evaluators should explain the purpose of the research done and feed back any provisional data collected for self analysis by trainees. This may, therefore, serve the objective of helping recipients of the training programme to achieve a gradual clarification of the process of learning. For Hesseling the facilitation of learning represents but one of the objectives that evaluation might serve. Dennis Pym is rather stronger on the correct purposes of evaluation: 'evaluation is the backbone of the learning and change process.'

Although Hesseling suggests that evaluators should be more open about the purpose of their research, he still assumes that it is for the evaluator to decide what research is to be conducted, and for the trainees to fall in with this design. Whether evaluators, and other researchers, should have the right to impose their designs upon others has been strongly questioned by a number of recent authors. And it can be argued that when learning is an explicit objective of educational research and evaluation, the research process should be truly collaborative involving both trainees and researchers in determining both what is to be done, and how it is to be done.

Deciding on the purpose of evaluation

In our experience it is not realistic to expect any evaluation to serve fully more than one of the three purposes outlined above, and this view is supported by Patton who stresses the importance of being specific about purposes. This assumes, of course, that the resources are limited in terms of people, time, and finance. It also provides a word of warning since it is so easy for evaluation to be conceived on an over ambitious scale which then results in nothing of consequence emerging from the effort involved. Perhaps it is possible for more than one purpose to be served if the questions to be answered are extremely limited, or if participants themselves take an extensive role in both the design and implementation of the evaluation. But for normal purposes it is important that an explicit choice should be attempted.

On the assumption that the person, or people, initiating some evaluation should attempt to clarify the purpose that their efforts are intended to serve, I have three suggestions about how they might go about this. These approaches I have labelled expediency; interests of stakeholders; and values of the evaluator.

Expediency

The approach of *expediency* assumes that the given activity is under some kind of threat, and that if this is so it may be worth trying to generate some information to demonstrate the value of it.

Interests of stakeholders

Another way into this dilemma is to identify the *mainstake-holder/client* of the evaluation and to infer what purpose he or she would like it to perform. Hesseling developed his 'typology of evaluations' based on the answers to two questions; evaluation *for whom*, and evaluation *by whom*. Under the former question he discusses the objectives and pre-requisites of each 'consumer of evaluation' when considering the results of training. These are as follows:

For *trainees* it would represent 'the last stage of a continuous learning process. In this sense evaluation can be seen as the interpretation of the learner's experience with new modes of behaviour'.

For the *trainers*, the main objectives of evaluation for the trainers is improvement of their training methods. ..(Their) learning from experience must be put on a more objective basis than intuition only'

For those involved in the supervision and *management of training*, typically expectations from evaluation research will be an indication what the critical points in training programmes are and how they can judge the performance of trainers and trainees'

Policy makers, whether in organisations or central government, will 'expect from evaluation research clarification of goals which can be reached by management training and a prognosis of the intended and unintended consequences of management training. They are interested in whether and how they have to allocate people, time and money to obtain optimal results from training programmes'

Scientists, and professional evaluators will expect 'evaluation studies to give insight into the dynamics of change underlying the effectiveness of the training programme'

Although one might disagree with some of the details of Hesseling's assumptions, they should provide some initial food for thought in considering alternative purposes. There is, of course, still the problem of identifying the main client of the study - and one of the case studies provided in Chapter 8 illustrates just how hard this may be particularly when the evaluator originates from outside the organisation.

Values of the evaluator

If there is no apparent threat to the programme, and no obvious pressures from clients and stakeholders, the evaluator may more easily be guided by his or her own *values and interests*. This is particularly so when the role of evaluator is being taken by a trainer or participants in the programme, and there is therefore no overt cost to the exercise. My impression is that those who are not unduly concerned by matters of expediency nor by pressures from stakeholders will tend to see *learning* as the most relevant purpose for evaluation. And there is some sense to this in that any attempt to gather data, regardless of purpose, will pace a burden upon informants; and if most of the information is to be provided by participants in the process it seems only fair that there should be some trade-off for them.

'Schools' of evaluation

Having thought a little about what kind of purpose the evaluation study can and should serve, it is worth considering the general approach to be adopted towards evaluation. In this area the literature is full of prescriptions, models, catch words, mnemonics and other forms of advice about how best to conduct evaluations. Rather than providing a long list, and descriptions of these approaches, we have attempted to group them into what may be termed the major 'schools of thought', and to classify them according to what appear to be the main underlying dimensions. These two dimensions, then *scientific naturalistic* dimension, and the *research-pragmatic* dimension are described below. we will then go on to discuss the main features of each of the schools of evaluation, what their limits are, and how they relate to this overall conceptual scheme.

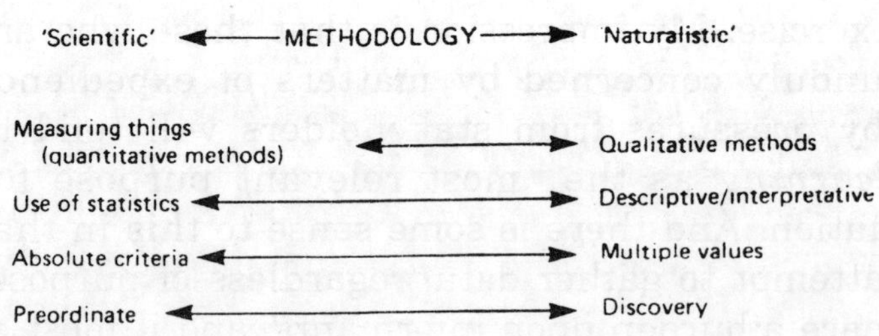

Figure: Contrasting methodologies

The first dimension, the scientific-naturalistic, involves distinctions that are essentially of *methodology*. The two extreme polls of this dimension are often referred to as distinct 'paradigms' which means, amongst other things, that they represent distinct, and largely incompatible, ways of seeing, and understanding, the world. This is so in theory, but in practice most evaluations contain elements of each stream, and therefore may be seen to reside somewhere on a more-or-less continuous dimension. There are normally analysed by statistical techniques in order to assess absolute criteria. In particular, the scientific approach prefers *preordinate* designs. That is, that the focus of the investigation, the measurement techniques and the ways of analysing these are determined as far as possible before any data are collected. This aspect contrasts strongly with the more 'naturalistic' methodologies, which emphasise the importance of discovering significant and important focuses for investigation as the study progresses, Correspondingly this type of methodology emphasises the use of qualitative methods for collecting data, thus enabling focusing and analysis at some later stage in, or after, the study. In making sense of this data it is also assumed that it may be assessed against many different value systems, and that none of these should necessarily be assumed as being more valid than others.

Whereas the first dimension of methodologies represent a debate that is extremely well worked out throughout the social sciences, the second dimension, that of contrasting styles, is of more specific relevance to the field of evaluation. The two extremes of this dimension, the 'research' style and the 'pragmatic' style, have been described elsewhere respectively as *Evaluation* and *evaluation*. The former was well represented in the early writings and advice on evaluation, and the scale and complexity of research-oriented evaluation styles may be one of the things that has put many people off the whole idea of evaluation. 'Research' styles stress the importance of *rigorous* procedures, whether the methodologies are essentially scientific or naturalistic. They stress that the direction, and emphasis of the evaluation study should be guided by theoretical considerations, and these considerations are aimed at producing enduring generalisations and knowledge about the learning and developmental processes involved. Whenever possible, the evaluator, who is normally assumed to be an independent person, is expected to maintain as much objectivity as possible about the courses under investigation. In contrast, the *pragmatic* approach emphasises reducing data collection and other time consuming aspects of the evaluation to the minimum possible level. The focus of the evaluation is determined by the practical interests of those who are involved in sponsoring it. And if these practical interests involve helping to make good operational decisions, for example, then the evaluation study will have served its purpose once such decisions have been taken provided they turn out to be reasonably correct in the long run. Characteristics of the two styles are illustrated.

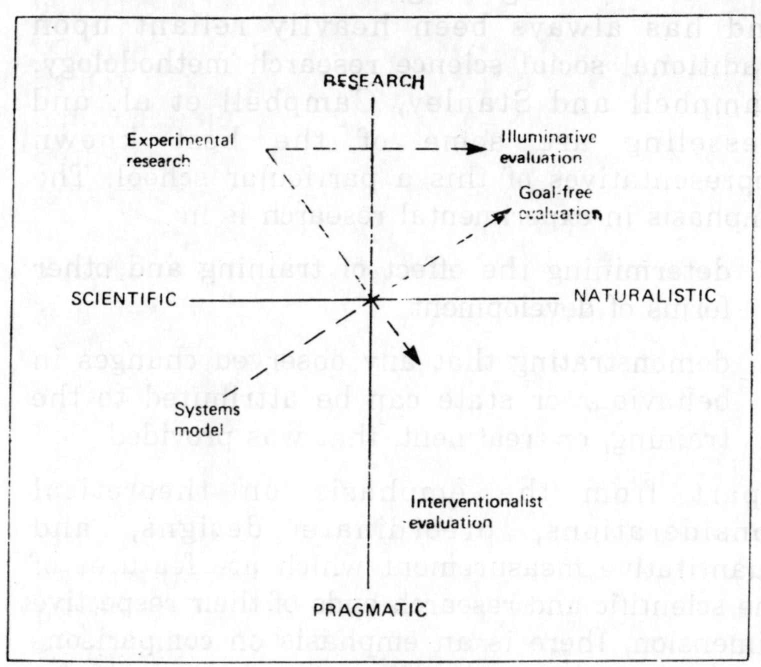

Figure: Models and schools of thought in evaluation

The discerning reader will by now have anticipated a graph with these two dimensions plotted out at right-angles to each other. While I would claim no 'scientific' validity to this particular graph we do find it of use in a 'pragmatic' sense to differentiate between some of the main features of the five main schools of evaluation which will be discussed belows. In addition to locating the 5 schools roughly within the two dimensions, dotted arrows have been included which indicate, and point to, the schools that have arisen primarily as a reaction to the school from which the arrow comes.

Experimental research

To start at the beginning, this school evolved first and has always been heavily reliant upon traditional social science research methodology. Campbell and Stanley, Campbell et al. and Hesseling are some of the best known representatives of this a particular school. The emphasis in experimental research is in:

1. determining the effect of training and other forms of development
2. demonstrating that any observed changes in behaviour or state can be attributed to the training, or treatment, that was provided.

Apart from the emphasis on theoretical considerations, preordinate designs, and quantitative measurement which are features of the scientific and research ends of their respective dimension, there is an emphasis on comparisons between the effects of different treatments. If, for example, the aim is to evaluate a supervisory training course which is intended to make supervisors more 'authentic' in their behaviour, the classic design would require a group of supervisors to be trained, and comparable group, matched who would not be trained during the same period. Individual supervisors would then be assigned on a random basis to one group or another, until sufficient numbers had been achieved, Both groups would then be measured on the scale 'authenticity', immediately before and after the training programme, and the difference in change between the two groups may then be attributed to the effect of the training programme. There are, of course, more elaborate designs involving multiple training groups which receive slightly different treatments, and multiple control groups which receive slightly different 'non-treatments', similarly, measurements may be taken a number of times before, during, and after the training programme in question.

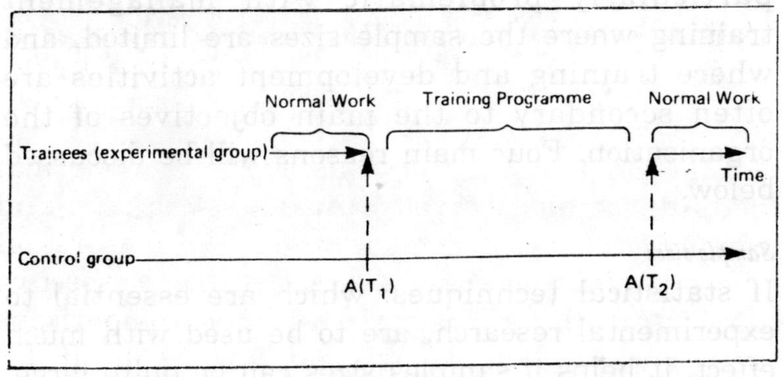

Figure : Comparative experimental research design

Nevertheless, the main features, are; comparisons between two or more groups, and measures before and after training.

The only problem is that it does not work particularly well in practice. For example, Hesseling provides a number of examples of this scientific research tradition being used to evaluate management training. Invariably the examples end with disclaimers, such as; 'the instruments were used and have to be tested in more situations and be refined before we can attain the accuracy and validity needed for drawing conclusions about the effectiveness of training' or 'we feel that research on a wider scale will have to be carried out in more organisations before the trainer can apply these instruments as normal tools in his work'. There are a number of reasons why this approach to evaluation does not work as well as it might, and although they apply to the evaluation of most forms of education they are particularly problematic with management training where the sample sizes are limited, and where training and development activities are often secondary to the main objectives of the organisation. Four main reasons will be discussed below.

Sample sizes

If statistical techniques. which are essential to experimental research, are to be used with much effect, it helps if samples sizes can be quite large. Even in secondary schools, where potential samples would almost seem to be infinite, it is often quite difficult in practice to achieve samples of sufficient size. It is even more so in management training when group sizes are often less than ten, and rarely more than thirty. And this suggests that an over-reliance upon discovering statistical significance when evaluating management training and development is unwise.

Control groups

Even if it is possible to obtain samples of sufficient size to generate statistical significance, there are innumerable problems in achieving genuine matching of control groups. In companies there are decisions about whether or not to train managers with the rest of management, and they are unlikely to accept the evaluator's request for randomised selection in order to meet the requirements of some obscure research design. Careful matching between those selected for training and members of a 'control' group drawn from a larger population of managers is more feasible politically, but even then it is hard to know upon which criteria to attempt the matching. For example, in one study conducted by myself some years' ago, a control group was selected by the management training manager (a psychologist) upon criteria of age, function, seniority, and assessed potential. It was not until after the results of the evaluation had been analysed that it was realised that all the managers selected to go on the programme had far closer relationships with their bosses than those who were not selected.

And there is a further difficulty with the notion of using matched control groups in evaluation. This is the assumption that 'no treatment', in this case no training, has a negligible impact upon those who form the control group- which is an extremely naive assumption, as those who have narrowly failed promotion boards, selection interviews, and other competitive features of the personnel machinery will be able to testify from their own experience.

Measurement

In general, there is a trade-off between the accuracy with which a variable can be measured and the significance of that particular variable. Thus it is possible to measure relatively trivial things with a fairly high degree of accuracy; but outcomes that might be thought to be of rather greater importance provides greater problems. In practice, it would be necessary to reduce the latter characteristic into more trivial, and measurable, terms, such as the ratio between positive and negative comments in appraisal documents. Alternatively this characteristic might be assessed according to reports from the subordinates in question - but the purist would no doubt claim that such holistic judgements are of dubious validity. The main problem here, of course, is that the general requirement for quantitative measurement tends to produce a trivialisation in the focus of the evaluation.

Causality

Although experimental designs are primarily intended to demonstrate causality between training developmental procedures and any subsequent outcomes it is often hard to isolate these procedures from other influences on the manager's behaviour. Considerations of why a particular manager has been chosen for a 'high flier' development scheme or for a redundancy counselling programme may have considerably more effect than the nature of the programmes themselves. And although it may be possible to reduce the impact of such 'irrelevant' influences in the case of tightly structured and programmed training, as discussed in the previous chapter, it becomes increasingly hard to determine the boundaries of complex developmental programmes.

Illuminative evaluation

The normal response of evaluators from the 'experimental research' school when faced with the limited success of their efforts, is to increase the sample, size, the statistical sophistication, and other features of scientific rigour.

Illuminative evaluation is generally used by its proponents with relatively small-scale programmes - and, as implied by the quotation above, most of these are with in schools or colleges. Although there is a fairly strong commitment to naturalistic and qualitative research methods., the use of questionnaires and attitude measurements is not explicitly ruled out. However, there is much emphasis on adopting a flexible, and open-ended approach to the research, as indicated by Ruddock's summary of the typical stages of illuminative evaluation. 'Generally, there are three stages; first, observation, further enquiry, attempts to explain; second, a progressive focus upon what appear to be key issues, often requiring extended interviews with participants; third, seeking general principles and placing findings within a broader explanatory context' Thus, to contrast this approach with the experimental research school, an illuminative evaluation of a management course aimed at developing greater 'authenticity' would not be greatly concerned to operationalise and measure the variable of authenticity. Instead it might focus upon the views of different people about what constitutes 'authentic behaviour' through open-ended interviews and tapes or transcripts of behaviour that were considered by some to show signs of authenticity. It might also focus upon who decided in the first place that 'authenticity' was a desirable characteristic possessed by managers in that organisation, and so on. Parlett recommends that the evaluator should attempt to be a 'neutral outsider' and should recognise that there may be multiple perspectives upon any particular issue selected. Parlett also comments upon what should be the proper purposes of illuminative evaluation 'to increase communal awareness' of a particular programme and processes involved, and the evaluator should not be troubled about the need to produce specific recommendations about future actions and improvements

It will be apparent from the above discussion that illuminative evaluation, although committed to a naturalistic methodology, is still seen primarily in research terms. One reason for this is that most studies have taken place in the area of education and social programmes, where funding arrangements may be quite liberal. There are, as yet, few published instances of illuminative evaluation being employed in a managerial training programme.

However, it seems that this emphasis on research has led to some concern about the usefulness of illuminative evaluation amongst a number of adherents to this particular school. Participants at the third Cambridge conference on naturalistic evaluation not only noticed that this form of evaluation had proved to be more costly than anticipated, but also that an unwarrantedly high proportion of evaluation reports based on this style had during the last few years been rejected by sponsors and other clients. A number of reasons where advanced by participants at the conference for why this should be so. Firstly, it was recognised that the naturalistic evaluators' rejection of psychometric methods which provide the impression of value-free measurement had led to evaluators becoming highly involved in the politics of their studies in some instances - and this had therefore reduced the willingness of clients and sponsors to place great reliance on evaluation results. There was also a suspicion that there was a mis-match of expectations between evaluators and clients. Whereas naturalistic evaluation methods are very good at demonstrating the complexity of educational processes, many sponsors and clients who have decision making responsibility would be hoping that the evaluation would simplify their task. And there was also the suspicion that whereas naturalistic evaluations generally aimed to present results in everyday language in order to improve communication, clients often show greater reverence to reports written in an alien scientific language which they do not understand. Finally, there was a feeling that naturalistic evaluation could not serve the interest of all the clients equally well, 'In practice those probably served best are the actors within the setting, who are closest to the problems and issues portrayed; the sponsors, on their account,.... are sometimes not served well. Other audiences are served even less well. The reality has fallen short of the aspiration'.

As with the 'experimental research' school, these problems with naturalistic evaluation have resulted in some members of the school redoubling their efforts to overcome them. rather than in rejecting some of the basic principles with which they are working. It does, however, point to the possibility of other 'schools' developing which have less of a research emphasis, and consequently where the role of evaluator is more likely to be taken on by teachers, trainers, or participants. This is particularly so of the systems model which has, for a long time, been the approach recommended to management trainers.

The systems model

Although there are many different glosses on the systems model, there are three main features which occur in the writings of authors who propose this kind of approach to evaluation; a concern to start with the *objectives;* an emphasis on identifying the outcomes of training; and a stress on proving *feedback* about these outcomes to those people involved in providing the inputs to training.

The need to start evaluation from the *objectives* of training is stressed by the UK

Department of Employment's Glossary of Training Terms, although in this case they use the word *validation,* and differentiate further between internal and external validation. Thus they define *internal validation* as 'a series of tests and assessments designed to ascertain whether a training programme has achieved the behavioural objectives specified'. *External validation* is, 'a series of tests and assessments designed to ascertain whether the behavioural objectives of an internally valid training programme were realistically based on an accurate initial identification of training needs in relation to the criteria of effectiveness adopted by the organisation'. *Evaluation* according to the Glossary is, 'the assessment of the total value of a training system, training course or programme in social as well as financial terms'. These definitions have been deeply ingrained in the practice of management trainers in the UK, particularly through the efforts of the Industrial Training Boards, I must also confess that they were one of the first things I learnt about evaluation, too. Nevertheless, the criticism was not slow in coming. Hamblin saw them on the one hand as being unnecessarily restrictive, and on the other hand in being over ambitious in recommending that the total value of training should be evaluated 'in social as well as financial terms'. But his own 'cycle of evaluation' is heavily dependent upon the formulation of objectives either as a starting point, or as a product of the evaluation process. Moreover his major *strategies* for evaluation are defined according to the level of objectives at which they commence. To do him credit, Hamblin also accepts in his model the need to look for the unanticipated,l as well as the anticipated, effects of training.

A second important features of Hamblin's work is the emphasis on measurement of *outcomes* from training at different levels. It is assumed that any training event, will, or can, lead to a chain of consequences, each of which may be seen as causing the next consequences. The important point stressed by Hamblin at this point is that it is unwise to conclude from unobserved change at one of the higher levels of effect that this was due to a particular training intervention, *unless* one has also followed the chain of causality through the intervening levels of effect. For example, it might be observed that a supervisors' approach to safety is markedly different from what it was six months' earlier just before she attended at training programme on safety. Hamblin would argue that unless it was possible to identify what she had learnt as a direct result of the training, and unless the training related directly to the changes in job behaviour it would not be wise to conclude that the training had this particular effect. Indeed, her change in behaviour might have been caused by a new managerial edict, by being closely involved with a serious accident in the plant, or by reading and thinking about the topic of safety for herself. Before leaving this example, it might be worth noting an interesting contrast between the relatively 'scientific' assumptions underlying the systems model of evaluation, and the way that this problem of causality would be approached by someone from the 'naturalistic' end of the methodological spectrum. Naturalistic evaluators would probably ask the supervisor directly to account for why she was now behaving in a different way, and might then check out the 'accuracy' of this interpretation by asking one or two of her close colleagues and subordinates for their views.

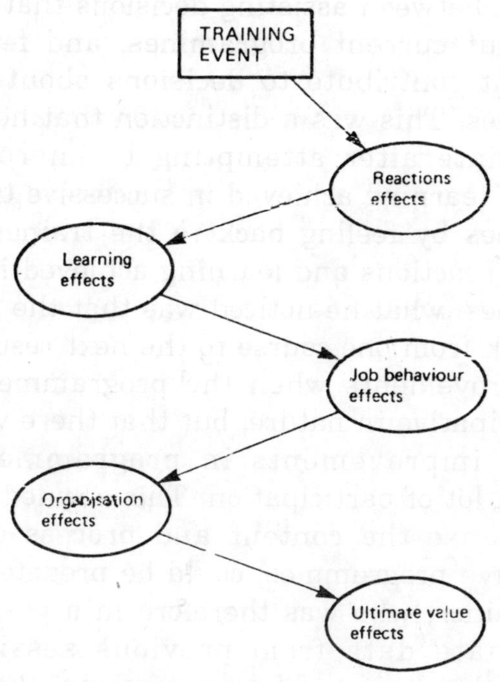

Figure: Chain of consequences for a training event

The third main feature of the systems model is the stress laid upon *feedback* to trainers and other decision makers in the training process. The process of feedback from effects to objectives is an essential idea in Hamblin's cycle of evaluation, and it also features significantly in the work of Warr, Bird, and Rackham. The latter authors take a particularly pragmatic view of evaluation suggesting that it should be of help to the trainer to make decisions about a particularly programme as it is happening, and most of the techniques that they recommend are relatively quick and easy to apply. Rackham subsequently makes a further distinction between assisting decisions that can be made about current programmes, and feedback that might contribute to decisions about future programmes. This was a distinction that he began to appreciate after attempting to improve the amount of learning achieved in successive training programmes by feeling back to the trainers data about the reactions and learning achieved in early programmes, what he noticed was that the process of feedback from one course to the next resulted in clear improvements when the programmes were non-participative in nature, but that there were no apparent improvements in programmes that involved a lot of participation. This seemed to him to be because the content and process of non-participative programmes, could be, predetermined by the trainer, who was therefore in a position to use evaluate data from previous sessions in adjusting the design of future sessions. But when the programme or session was designed on a participative basis, this meant that some element of control and direction was inevitably vested in the hands of the learners; consequently its course could not be fully predetermined by the trainer, and therefore the evaluative data possessed by the trainer about previous sessions that he had run would not be so easily usable. The approaches aimed at providing feedback for decisions about the current programme and for decisions about future programme were labelled short cycle and long cycle evaluation respectively.

The idea of feed back as an important aspect of evaluation was developed further in a later paper by Burgoyne and Singh. First of all they distinguished between evaluation as feedback, and evaluation adding to a body of *knowledge*. The former they saw as providing transcient and perishable data relating directly to decision making, and the latter they saw as generating permanent and enduring knowledge about education and training processes:

1 *Intra-method decisions* about how particular methods are handled, for example 'lectures' may vary from straight delivery to lively debates between the lecturer and his/her audience.

2 *Method decisions*. for example, whether to employ a lecture, a case study, or a similation in order to introduce the topic of 'business ethics'.

3 *Programme decisions*: about the design of particular programmes, whether they should

be longer or shorter, more or less structured, taught by insiders or visiting speakers, and so on.

4. *Strategy decisions*: about the optimum use of resources, and about the way the training institution might be organised.
5. *Policy decisions*: about the overall provision of funding and resources, and the role of the institution as a whole, whether for example, a management training college should see itself as an agent for change or as something that oils the wheels of changes that are already taking place.

The above examples of applications of the systems model have all been drawn deliberately from the evaluation of training. This is because the systems model has been given such widespread application to training within the UK. As we have seen above, there are numerous examples of it being used similarly in the USA and it has also been used quite extensively in other contexts.

Notwithstanding the widespread use and acceptance of the systems model, there are a number of problems and limitations that should be understood by those who choose to use this approach. These can be related directly to the three main features discussed above, and we shall take them in their reverse order now. Firstly, the main limitation with the notion of feedback is what we call the 'systems fallacy'. This is that data provided from evaluations of what has happened in the past can only contribute marginally to decisions about what should happen in the future: logically they can only contribute to incremental adjustments based on the past designs, and cannot in themselves indicate whether any more radical changes should be made in the future. For example, a systems-based evaluation of an executive programme might indicate which visiting speakers were liked, and which were not. This data is obviously useful to a course director in deciding whether or not to invite certain individuals back to the next course; but it cannot tell him who to invite instead, nor could it tell him whether he should scrap the whole idea of visiting speakers in favour of establishing a self-development learning community for these executives. In order to arrive at this more radical change the programme director would need either to gather data from outside the existing programme. or to indulge in some of the more creative evaluative processes suggested by Patton.

Likewise, the emphasis on outcomes provides a good and logical approach to evaluation, but it must be recognised that it represents a mechanistic view of learning. In an extreme form it assumes that learning consists of placing facts and knowledge in people's heads in the hope that this will become internalised, before gradually becoming incorporated in their behavioural responses. This view might be adequate when training salesmen how to get a better response from 'cold calls', or how to interpret a balance sheet: but it makes little sense with some of the more complex and experiential forms of learning.

What, for example, is the chain of consequences when a manager on a self-development programme suddenly realises that his family life is being overwhelmed by the structures of his working life, and he therefore needs to establish a much greater sense of balance between the activities to which he devotes his energy?

Finally, the emphasis on starting with *objectives* brings us to one of the classic critiques of the systems approach. This is the question: whose objective are they? Are the correct objectives of training defined by the organisation, by the trainers, by the trainees' bosses, by the trainee, or by some external validating body?As we have indicated above these may differ quite markedly, and the 'formal' objectives of a particular programme may represent a gross oversimplification. Moreover, it is questioned by a number of authorities whether there is any particular value in specifying formal objectives at all, since among other things, this might place undue restrictions on the learning that could be achieved from a particular educational or training experience.

Goal free evaluation

The issue of whether or not evaluation should start with a consideration of the objectives of training and education leads directly to the next major evaluation school; that of goai free evaluation. In particular, goal free evaluation starts from the assumption that the evaluator should avoid consideration of formal objectives in carrying out his or her work. It was Michael Scriven, who was credited with proposing the radical view that the evaluator should take no notice of the formal goals and objectives of a programme when carrying out an investigation of it. In practice this might involve trying to avoid contact with a course director before and during the programme, and deliberately not looking at course brochures or proposals to validating bodies. Instead the evaluator should spend his time talking to participants and other stakeholders, and should attempt to observe carefully what takes place during and after the programme. Only in this way, argues Scriven, can the evaluator avoid being contaminated by those who have vested interests in the programme - and this is essential if he is to form a balanced judgement about the real *value* of it.

A similar line is adopted by Deutscher in pointing out the dangers of basing evaluation studies on the formal goals of programmes. For a start, he argues, the formal goals of a programme are often framed in order to attract funding, or participants, and they may represent only a small part of what the tutors hope that the programme will achieve. If the evaluator focuses his or her attention on these formal goals the study may only pick up a small part of what actually happens on the programme. Deutscher makes three suggestions about how to deal with, what he calls, the 'goal trap'. First he advise the evaluator to discuss with all interested parties what they would consider to be reasonable objectives for the programme. This should provide a far wider basis for judging the value or otherwise, of the programme. Second, even if a range of objectives is taken into account, there is still a danger that the evaluation will concentrate on what was generally expected at the beginning of the programme to transpire subsequently, and it therefore may not notice any changes in direction if they happen during a programme. To guard against this, Deutscher advises the evaluator to look specifically for *unanticipated* outcomes. Third, he suggests that the whole concentration upon outcomes is itself unhealthy. Although some interest in outcomes may obviously be necessary, the evaluator is advised to pay greater attention to the processes which take place within the programme and the experiences of participants before during and after its completion. In practice this might involve observing planning meetings, discussing with various stakeholders their objectives and expectations at different stages in the programme mixing socially with participants,and interviewing them some time after the programme has been completed.

In view of the last point, it will be seen that goal free evaluation generally demonstrates more of a preference for naturalistic methods. The implicit assumption in most discussions about goal free evaluation is that the evaluator will normally be an outsider; indeed, those individuals closely involved with the programme would theoretically find their roles incompatible with the conduct of goal free evaluation. Some readers may feel this is a gross generalisation. but it does seem that goal free evaluation does not necessarily have such an important research emphasis as illuminative evaluation, and there are indeed examples of some of the principles of goal free evaluation being used in a relatively pragmatic way. Jameson provides an example of a relatively successful goal free evaluation of a course for small business people which was carried out by herself, one of the major stakeholders. Although in cases like this, as Patton points out, there is always the danger that the approach will simply substitute the evaluator's goals for those of the trainees and other stakeholders.

Like many of the evaluation styles which use naturalistic methods, goal free evaluation is intended to be of relevance to 'decision requirements', but the research assumption implicit in this style mean that it is likely to be most useful when considering innovative programmes where significant funding is available.

Interventionalist evaluation

There are many labels that have been applied to evaluation approaches falling within this general group; decision orientated, client orientated, barefoot, utilisation-focussed, and responsive evaluations, to name but a few, I shall concentrate on the latter two in this section because they are reasonably well represented, and their principles are quite widely disseminated.

Firstly, Stake helps to locate this general

'school' by contrasting a responsive evaluation with the preordinate approach of *experimental research*. A preordinate evaluation requires the design to be clearly specified and determined before evaluation begins, it makes use of 'objective' measures, evaluates these against criteria determined by programme staff, and produces results in the form of research-type reports. In contrast, responsive evaluation focuses upon programme activities rather than intentions, and takes account of the different value perspectives involved. Both of these features, it may be recognised, are shared with goal free evaluation, as described above. In addition, however, Stake stresses the importance of attempting to respond to the audience's requirements for information, and this contrasts somewhat with the attempts by certain goal free evaluators to distance themselves from some of the principle stakeholders in the programme that is to be evaluated. Stake is also more catholic in his recommendations about evaluation methods, and recognises that 'the different styles of evaluation will serve different purposes'. He also recognizes that preordinate evaluations may be preferable to responsive evaluations under certain circumstances - for example, if clients generally wish to check upon goal attainment. We find it more useful to construct two dimensional figures which contain some inherent contractions than to have all the possible contradictions and distinctions mapped out onto a whole series of separate axes.

To continue with the pragmatic line, Patton

also recognises that there is a range of techniques, both quantitative and qualitative, which may be used to advantage in evaluation studies. Indeed, he is less concerned with issues of methodological rigour and correctness, than he is with the problem of getting the questions right. In this, he stresses that it is essential to find out precisely that information the decision maker needs in order to make whatever decisions are necessary This is both a matter of helping the client to clarify his or her own mind before and during the programme but also agreeing with the client about what interpretations might be placed upon different kinds of result from study. For example, if 20 per cent of participants on a management and training programme said they 'got a lot', and if the remaining 80 per cent said they 'got a little' from the programme is that to be interpreted as a good result, or a bad result; and if it is a bad result, just how had is it?

This emphasis on prior agreement with the client may be seen to conflict with Stake's view of responsive evaluation. But it is only a superficial conflict, because Patton's emphasis on discussing the design and interpretation with the client introduces a significant response feature; and it is also recognised that the client may develop and reformulate his questions as the study proceeds. A final point about this approach to evaluation, which is discussed by both Stake and Patton is that traditional research-type reports are not necessarily particularly helpful. Clients tend to be more impressed by what is known as 'face validity' than the more strictly determined notions of a scientific validity. They also tend to find reports easier to use if they are written in everyday language, as opposed to the dry scientific jargon that is used in traditional reports. This contradicts somewhat with the view expressed by Jenkins *et al*. That many clients really prefer evaluation reports to be written in scientific language. Perhaps the difference between illuminative and interventionalist evaluation in relation to this point is that addition to 'user-friendly' language the latter form of evaluation approach is also likely to be addressing directly the questions that the client would like to have addressed.

The reason why I have grouped this range of approaches, which may seem to some to be quite disparate under the general heading of interventionalist evaluation to have the direct impact upon programmes and those involved with them. It is this form of *confrontation* that Critten, based on his recent Ph.D Thesis, argues is the very essence of evaluation 'Until parties involved personally confront the data emerges through the purposes we have described, they will be unable to *full release* the value inherent in that experience'. On a similar line, Patton comments: 'Finally is utilisation-focused evaluation the underlying and constantly recurring analysis or interpretation issue is how to translate the findings into action... Utilisation-focused evaluation is aimed at producing knowledge that makes a difference, that is actually used'.

The main strengths of interventionalist evaluation approaches should now be apparent. They are likely to be perceived to be relevant by decision makers, and possibly other stakeholders, and are also likely to be realistic about the resources required to provide usable results. It is claimed that they are more 'honest' and less alienated than other approaches to evaluation, particularly compared to those that rely heavily on scientific methods. But as we have seen above this claim is dependent upon how it is seen by clients and others, and their rational views of the evaluator. Finally the interventionalist styles, particularly responsive evaluation, are more likely to be flexible and adaptive to changing situations and processes as they take place during and around a particular programme.

The potential weaknesses of interventionalist evaluation approaches are closely linked to the above strengths. One danger is that this form of evaluation can become too flexible, adapting and changing to every passing whim and circumstances, and therefore producing results and conclusions that are weak and inconclusive. Another problem is that the evaluator who tries to develop a close relationships with clients and other participants may become too involved with the programme itself, thus sacrificing some impartiality and the credibility that comes with this. This is, of course, the problem that goal free evaluation sets out to avoid. Clearly there is no definitive solution to this dilemma but it is something that the evaluator, whether an insider or an outsider to particular programme, should be aware of and should seek to maintain in appropriate balance.

Choosing an evaluation style

By this stage the reader may be becoming overwhelmed by the range of evaluation approaches and styles that are available. However, the aim of this chapter has been to demonstrate that there are a great many starting points, assumptions and purposes that may be covered by evaluation - and that evaluators should not necessarily take a particular style for granted. What, therefore, should be evaluator do when faced with this wide range of choice, yet needing to make a decision about adopting one overall approach, or another?

The following observations relate to the general dimensions illustrated in Figure 2.5, and the reader might then be able to relate them specific features of the evaluation styles described above - particularly, as I have tried to emphasise, when there exists a considerable range of approaches and methods within any single style, especially from the viewpoint of different proponents of this style.

First, there is the question of the relationship between purposes and styles. It should be clear from the above discussion that there is no necessary relationships between the two, for example, a goal-free evaluation or an interventionalist evaluation may be aimed at *proving*, just as much as an experimental research evaluation. Similarly, examples of experimental research might be intended to facilitate *learning* just as much as the systems model of illuminative evaluation. Nevertheless, based on the apparent values, and experiences, of proponents from different schools and styles my assumption is that studies aimed to fulfil the purpose *proving* will tend to be located near the 'research' end of the dimension, and studies aimed at *improving* will tend to be located near the 'pragmatic' end. On the methodological dimension there may be more concern with *proving* at the 'scientific' end, and *learning* at the 'naturalistic' end.

There are other more practical considerations that might help in the choice of an appropriate evaluation style. If there is no *funding* available to support an evaluation activity, then there is little option but to adopt a 'pragmatic' style; 'research' styles can be extremely costly in terms of time and money. My own experience of naturalistic approaches, particularly when they rely heavily on qualitative methods, is that they can be far more time-consuming than some of the quantitative methods employed in 'scientific' approaches. The analysis of quantitative data can be highly automated nowadays, whereas qualitative data still requires much painstaking attention from evaluators.

Apart from this, the choice between 'scientific' and 'naturalistic' approaches is often one of personal preference and expertise. But the fashion has been swinging from the former to the latter during the 1970s, and I suspect that it may swing in the other direction during the 1980s. This is because of the tighter constraints being placed upon expenditure in countries throughout the world, and the consequent pressures to justify activities and programmes in terms of measurable outcomes. And whether or not this will result in a renewed predominance of quantitative methods is largely a matter of what will be considered as credible and useful by those people who have significant stakes in management education and development - this, of course, betrays my own preference for the more 'pragmatic' forms of evaluation!

Of the three contexts to be discussed in this chapter, management *education* invites consideration at the most macro level. Policies for management education are very frequently the concern of national governments, or of powerful national foundations, associations, or institutions. With this in mind it is often very difficult to separate policy issues from the interests of individuals, groups, or political organisations.

The questions that may be asked of management education at a policy level therefore tend to vary very much with the interests of those who are doing the questioning. Thus national governments, which frequently tend to be in the funding role are likely to be concerned with issues of cost-effectiveness. At this crudest level this may be measured by the number of diplomas, MBAs, or PhDs produced, for every pound or dollar, pumped into the education system. A second group of crucial stakeholders for management education, are the organisations which are likely to become the future employers of business graduates, and which also provide the managers who attend shorter post-experience programmes within the educational system. Here the primary concerns, or questions, are likely to be about relevance: whether the skills and abilities supposedly learnt within educational institutions are really likely to contribute to the overall effectiveness of the employing organisation - does it really contribute to the 'bottom line'? For the third major group of stakeholders, the educational institutions, the policy questions are likely to centre on the best mix and range of programmes or activities which will contribute to *their* overall reputation, prestige, and financial viability.

Evaluation methods at this policy level tend to be surprisingly 'naturalistic'. The normal practice is to employ consultants, or to establish working parties and commissions which travel around the country soliciting opinions from a sample of reliable observers or informants. There are two reasons for why this is so. Firstly, one is clearly dealing with questions on such a wide scale that unless the main focus can be narrowed down very precisely, there are so many intervening variables that more 'scientific' approaches simply could not be cope with when measuring this enormous diversity and scale. The second is that a this level it is quite pointless trying to disguise the political nature of decisions being made, and therefore it seems quite acceptable to use overtly the kind of information that most senior decision makers really rely on - informed opinions, from people whom they trust and respect.

There have been a number of critiques of management education produced both in the USA and the UK, by authors with wide experience of the respective systems, but without the adoption of any very clear evaluation methodology such as making an attempt to identify a reasonably balanced sample of 'informed' observers. In Britain, the classic evaluation of management education, was commissioned by the British Institute of Management and the Confederation of British Industry in 1970, and published in 1971. This investigation was prompted by concerns from major industrial organisations that the business schools had moved into providing highly academic forms of management education, rather than the more practical and skills-oriented education that was assumed to be of greater relevance to British industry. The investigators, led by Trevor Owen, formerly a Personnel Director of ICI, visited 53 firms in manufacturing industries and talked to senior managers both in personnel and operating functions. The report, and its conclusions, were based on a consensus of 'considered opinion' from those people surveyed. Predictability, the report confirmed many of he existing criticisms of management education in the UK up to that time: there was too much emphasis on academic courses; and the selection of students on to those courses was based on academic criteria rather than potential managerial ability and graduates from their courses usually had an inflated view of their own abilities, assuming that they were already jut a short step from the Managing Director's seat. Given the sample from which these views are solicited, the conclusions of the Owen Report were not surprising, but they were influential; and that is the way of much evaluation at this level.

One of the activities within business schools which has come under considerable scrutiny over the years in the MBA - and a whole range of questions are asked about it such as: does it result in any significant changes in people who follow an MBA; to what extent are the holders of MBAs better or worse than other managers without MBAs; do MBAs, as institutions, provide a social function in maintaining the dominance of business and managerial elites in the face of economic and technological change? One major study, intended to identify the effect of the MBAs provided by a range of business schools in different countries was commissioned by the European Foundation for Management Development in the early 1970s. The basic design required the monitoring of a complete year's intake to the MBA programmers in eight institutions in six different countries, and following the progress of those students over a period of two years. A very extensive battery of psychometric measures and questionnaires was assembled and administrated to all students at the beginning of their courses, and these were repeated at the end of a period of one year. An attempt was also made to obtain matched control groups for all of the students by asking each one on the MBA programme to nominate a friend of his or hers who was not on the programme, but who was similar in ability, personality, and general career progress. This led to one rather interesting result, as we shall see in a moment.

Measures for this evaluation were chosen largely on the basis of their known reliability, rather than because they were thought to be highly appropriate to the skills and attributes that MBAs were supposed to be generating in those students. This choice of measures led to one extraordinary incident when the results of the 16PF tests were being compared between a number of institutions in different countries. A working group had been making considerable progress over a day and a half in producing some interesting interpretations of the difference exhibited between English and Italian students. Progress was being made...until one of the researchers suddenly realised that the scoring protocol for the 16PFs completed by the Italian students was based on the English version of the test, which used both a different language *and* structure. Therefore this working group had spent over a day developing what they thought were very meaningful interpretations from data which were shown to be completely random.

This is the first cautionary tale from this particular study; the second is that the overall results were failing to demonstrate any positive effect from the MBA programmes and a decision was taken not to publish any of the reports from the working party. The one unpublished manuscript that has come into my possession was based primarily on the data gathered at Manchester Business School. This part of the survey was unable to identify any significance differences in a sample of MBA students over the one year period of study; but more seriously, it found that the MBA students indicated rather less overall adjustment, than the control group who were not attending the MBA, but who for the most part were working in industry. Perhaps this provides, at last, some more quantitative evidence to support the views expressed in the Owen report. But then, that is how things were in the 1970s, and to be fair, most of the MBA programmes have changed very significantly since those days.

Management training policies

In this context there is once again some difference between the nature of policy issues considered at a national level, and those considered at the company or organisation level. At a national level, concern about the nature and extent of management training varies somewhat with political priorities and the existence of national bodies and institutions that regard themselves as being responsible for promoting it.

Within the UK during the last two decades national policy on management training, such as it has existed, has been greatly dominated by the Industrial Training Boards, the Training Services Agency, and the Manpower Services Commission. However, each of these was not set up primarily to service the needs of *management* training, and the extent to which they have taken any interest in this area has been result of the initiatives and pressures of concerned individuals and groups. Also, the emphasis has changed somewhat over time as political and economic pressures have changed. For example, the Manpower Services Commission was set up in the mid-1970s to co-ordinate national policy on employment and on industrial training. At that time the main interests in management training were in the areas of up-dating skills for managers, thus providing greater mobility in the workforce, and in stimulating within companies the roles of management raining and management development advisers. This latter aspect probably derived from the fact that many of the Industrial Training Boards had invested a considerable amount of resources over the years in such advisory roles. However, as unemployment became more and more of a political issue in Britain, the priorities regarding management training shifted towards the provision of courses for redundant executives, and towards a range of initiatives intended to create new successful small businesses.

At the level of industrial companies and organisations, the policy issues have less obvious political impact, although obviously the range of debate and questions are rather more diverse. As with the case with national policy, at a company level, policy issues are also largely the concern of those at the top - in this case, top manages, directors of training establishments, and senior personnel managers. Burgoyne provides an interesting overview of many of the theoretical issues that may be involved in consideration of management development policies within companies. in practical terms some of the questions that may be asked and which reflect on company training policy are:

Should management training be run within the company, or contracted out to other organisations, or scrapped altogether?

If management training is to be run within companies should this be set up as a profit centre which charges commercial rates to al participants or as a cost centre which is effectively subsidised by the company's central financial resources?

Should such a management training college be staffed by line managers on secondment, or by 'professional' trainers, or by a mixture of both?

Should management training be proved for distinct strata in the organisation, thus reinforcing the identity of different levels, or should it concentrate on particular skill or topics, thus perhaps reinforcing the notion of a 'task' culture?

In many companies there is considerable resistance to the idea of proving training programmes for managers at different levels. One example of this particular barrier being broken recently occurred in British Airways when, as a result of staffing cutbacks, particularly in clerical grades, a group of very senior managers were sent off on a typing course.

There are other policy issues *how* management training should be conducted and organized. For example, should an emphasis be placed upon providing training *away* from the job, or should this be integrated as closely as possible with the manager's normal job. Another major dilemma for management training policies, particularly during periods of rapid environmental change, is whether management training should be attempting to *push* new ideas and approaches on managers, or whether it should take a more low-key role of supporting the *status quo* and simply responding to initiatives for change which emerge from the top of the organization.

One recent example of this form of evaluation is provided by the report of the Institute of Manpower Studies, Sussex University, into the operation of the Youth Training Scheme (YTS). One of the main themes of this report, which was based on extensive interviewing with both providers and 'clients' of YTS schemes was about just what is meant by the term ' skill ownership'. If managers are being trained the public expense should they themselves be seen as the rightful owners of the skills that they obtain from the training, or should they have some obligation to use them to contribute either to employing organisations or to the communities in which they live. Furthermore, should training programmes have an obligation to concentrate on skills that may be of use in one context or another?

Thus, in this way an evaluation study may contribute to debates by focusing on the dilemmas that underlie specific policy decisions. And furthermore, they may also contribute to achieving some consensus over the criteria against which such training programmes might be judged subsequently - although no doubt in the time-honoured way through collecting informed opinions from reliable observers/participants!

Another example in which evaluation was used to contribute to debates on management training policy was carried out by myself and some colleagues in major multi-national. Again this was seen largely within the context of *improving*, and semi-structured interviews were conducted with a sample of about thirty managers attending programmes at the company's international Management Education Centre. These interviews focused both on their jobs and on how the nature and problems of these jobs was changing; and how they felt their training experience was relating, and should relate, to such changes. The report derived from this study also crystallised a number of issues that needed to be considered in future policy formulation. One of these was the need to devise procedures for adapting the training experience to the very different problems and dilemmas faced by the individuals drawn from perhaps a dozen totally different countries. Another product from this study was an attempt to clarify how managers' roles can change evolve quite significantly over time within their normal work - thus helping to focus any problems of 'transfer' into a more dynamic view of the jobs of the manager in the normal work environment.

Management development policies

At the policy there is considerable overlap between management development and management training - at least within a single organization. The questions that may be asked are of the same kind, even though they may have a slightly different focus. One frequent question is whether the organisation should take responsibility for the career development of all manages, or whether some elite cadre of managers should be given special treatment by being placed on the 'fast track'. Furthermore, if a fast track policy is decided upon, should the associated assessment career development system be an open one; or should it be a closed system, where not only the names of those on the high flier list are kept secret, but also the existence of the system itself is supposed to be kept secret? And indeed, it is quite surprising just how frequently senior managers both prefer close systems and also believe that they are being kept secret.

The above two examples relate to what might be termed the 'technical' aspects of management development, where it is regarded largely as a separate activity from the mainstream managing of the organisation. However, recent thinking in the United States has regarded management development as being much more closely integrated with the management style and value systems of the organisation as a whole. Peters and Waterman are probably the most prominent voices in this respect, and they place considerable emphasis upon the development of clearly understood value systems, and the establishment of very supportive climates which try to make most managers and employees feel that they are doing an excellent job.

One implication of this kind of philosophy is that any appraisal systems which are intended to provide feedback on performance to managers and employees should be designed in such a way that most of the information feedback is very positive. Another clear implication is that the main responsibility for building such a climate and ensuring that positive feedback takes place lies entirely with managers from the top to the bottom of the organisation - rather than with any personnel or management development specialists. Another influential advocate of this kind of philosophy is Lewis Lehr, the Chairman of the 3M Company. He even goes as far as to encourage, and even honour, those who make mistakes within the company - on the grounds that this is the bet way of helping managers to take risks and thereby increasing the ability of the organisation to learn from its actions. He has but one reservation to this philosophy: 'We expect any mistakes to have originality. We can afford almost any mistake once'.

So what contribution might evaluation make in this area? Firstly with regard to the more technical aspects of management development policies there is a role for evaluation in finding out what the effects of those policies are 'on the ground floor'. This is one thing that the management development audit attempts to do in a general way across the whole spectrum of training and development activities. Such relative activity could be rather more focused, for example one might wish to enquire into the effect that the existence of a 'fast track' system has on managers at different stages of their careers. In this case a few careful discussions with selected managers (qualitative interviews), may well suffice. For example, one of the classic problems with such systems was pinpointed by a comment from a middle manager whom I interviewed in one such study a few years ago: 'But you see, the people it really screws up are those like me who just failed to get in'.

This leads to the second main role that evaluation may play in this area which is to stimulate people to ask the right questions about aspects of the organization and the way it treats managers, and to provide some contribution to the debate about those questions. In this case it puts evaluation into the role of offering an interactive dialogue with policy makers, who have responsibility for running the company.

6 How Can We Understand Organisations?

The development of theories about organisations in the last 60 to 70 years shows a distinct move from a view that organisations are inherently impersonal structures towards the view that organisations are essentially collections of people with individual needs and contributions. Organisation theories almost always derive from problems of management and are more properly called management theories since they concern themselves with how organisations can be better 'organised' or managed. The impetus for researching about organisations has arisen from the need to solve management problems concerning matters such as rewards, motivation, control and leadership. In order to gain general acceptability, organisation theories are made to pass the test of being apparently practical-the term indicates a way to better practice. While it is by no means unreasonable to expect theories to have application, the changes in theory lead one to wonder if there have ever been any truly fundamental theories of management/organisation or only abstract solutions to problems as currently perceived in accordance with the contemporary cultural values.

The definition quality of a theory is that it provides an internally coherent way of looking at phenomena in a described field so that the generalisations of the theory can be applied in specific cases. The terms of the application are consistent, inherent in the theory and special to the specific instance. Yet all *management* theory generalises from the particular to the general; nearly all *organisation* theory generalises from hypothetical solutions to management problems. These statements appear to be true of, for example Weber's theory of bureaucracy, the administrative theory of Chester Barnard, the Socio-Technology theory of Trist and the Tavistock and Norwegian schools, and the pragmatism of all business managers.

What are the problems for developing a theory

There seems little doubt of the need to develop some basic theory of organisations; a base or ground upon which an understanding of organisations can be developed and which will give some unity and integrity to what people write about organisations. There have been only a few attempts to provide basic concepts to thinking about organisations perhaps the most important of which has been general systems theory. The advantage of general systems theory is that it applies to other areas of investigation than formal human organisation and provides a supposedly value-free framework for investigation. However, the social-scientists concerned with looking at organisations and using general systems theory have in every case jumped from a value-free framework of organisations as open systems to a value-laden interpretation of the nature of human systems. For the systems concept to be valued for examining human organisation we should need to know what actually are the systems and subsystems that exist and this would require an analysis not unlike that required for the identification of species of plants. As it is, systems theories of organisation always *assume* the reality of the systems and subsystems described and pre-determined the descriptive categories such as leadership, product, control and so on, or local, regional and national systems.

At its crudest, the systems model of the school takes graphic view of the school as the central subsystem of concentric circles of larger environmental meta-systems. Even the term 'environment' is used in a contentious manner which assumes that organisation environments are external to one another even though they act upon them. Of course, a simplistic systems model may well be useful for ordering the chapters in a book or sorting out priorities in a research project but the open systems concept of input, throughput and output are not even adequately descriptive of the sausage making process let alone human membership of organisations. The use to which the general systems theory of organisations has been put has invariably involved changing the organisation towards a desired direction by assuming that there is a particular, reasonably clear primary tasks and thus task almost always turns out to be related to the organisation qua organisation rather than the members as people. In all the systems descriptions, there is an assumption that the organisation has preeminence over the membership though with the tendency for personal identification with the organisational task to increase up the managerial hierarchy to the boss - where interests are perceived as identical with those of the organisation. Although systems theory points out that all organisations are part of other organisations and hence are dependent on them in some way, the influence of the external environment is generally considered to be more *important* than the needs of the sub-organisation. In short, users of general systems theories of organisations soon interpose values and the question arises as to whether systems theories of organisations have any basic categories of analysis that are essentially neutral in significance.

The extention of the question is, is there a theory of organisations that is, or can be, essentially value free and if not, are there alternatives? The problem is one of observation, description and analysis. Can human behaviour be observed in any way that is not biased so that even if categories could be devised for description, could bias or interpretation be avoided? At the present time it seems unlikely that there is any possibility of making objective observations of human behaviour; even the choice of categories is subjective and selective, the observer being too much a part of the culture he observes. Human behaviour is always complex with several motives and reasons present at any time. A simple examples is the 'observation' that two people are crossing the road the significance of the act and awareness will be quite different for each of them. For a blind persona highly charged and dangerous situation; for a teenage lad intent on meeting his girlfriend hardly any awareness of crossing a busy st' eet. However apparently similar the acts may be, their significance is different; any truly scientific observation would be concerned with such significance.

If we use the kind of categories that are currently used in organisation theory we have not only categories that can only be useful if they are "properly" interpreted but categories the significance and definition of which have not been adequately determined. For instance, we use terms like "motivation" and "leadership" as aspects of orgnisational behaviour but motivation is something that can only exist within the person motivated while leadership relates to bahaviour of a number of individuals. There has been no attempt to define and relate the terminology used in talking about organisations to proper scientific categories. The social sciences abound in semantic difficulties, and, of course, of course, it is more than likely that such scientific is not appropriate. For example, the social sciences tend to use mathematical and statical formulae in an idiosyncratic way. Mathematical relationships are deemed to indicate relationships between phenomena in a way that is often logically improper. Observations are assumed to be accurate when, as has been illustrated above, the 'observations' are little more than speculative deductions. The need for the social sciences to demonstrate their credibility by using the formulae from true sciences is by now pathological. Literary criticism, religious studies, law, language studies, history find no need to quantify so relentlessly and appear none the worse and to be held in no less esteem. It seems almost ridiculous that organisation theory which is demonstrably pragmatic in the vent and has so clearly failed to be either scientific or logical should persist in its image as a pseudo-science. Clearly we need to look in some other direction for credibility and validity.

Things are what they seem

The one fact about organisation that is self-evident is that everyone sees his organisation is a different way from everyone else. Teachers and pupils view schools differently from one another as members of categories and also as individuals. In fact, in term,s of their view of the school, "teacher" and "pupil" are unlikely to be valid categories indicating discrete differences except on specified dimensions. A head may view things differently from his subordinates; his subordinates may not even perceive themselves as subordinates. We may of course try to redefine categories and redefine our definitions but the more we do thus, the less manageable the information. Redefining species and subspecies of plants is a different matter since we are dealing with permanent differences; with human beings as members of organisations there are no inherent and permanent differences. To try to look at organisations from outside appears to be a hopeless task. But it is equally difficult to try to gather information from within the organisation, since in doing this the investigator often does not make hypotheses which he tests, he makes assumptions which he seems to confirm For example, let us take the idea of organisational climate. It seems quite logical to assume that organisations have emotional or psychological climates - after all, families do; some are 'friendly', others are 'tense'. But then these terms are statements of my response to the situation, not necessarily that of the members. They are subjective interpretations. All right, so what if we ask the members what they feel about the organisation can we still say that the climate of the organisation is 'friendly'! Only if everyone not only says just that, but also means the same thing by it. However, what do we do with this data when we have collected it? Will it still be valid and for how long? Is 'friendliness' a characteristic of the climate or a response to other things that occur - such as having a lot of personal friends as colleagues, even if one hates the boss. Furthermore, in collecting data about climate, the researcher will almost certainly have decided which climates he approves of and of which he disapproves. The fact that a climate may be neither generally friendly nor unfriendly just isn't in his book of rules.

What can be known?

Can we, then, know nothing? Is there no reality?

It looks rather as if the only reality is the perceived reality of the individual, whoever he is. What is real for me may not be real for anyone else - and reality is what I believe to be real, that to which I react. This is an existentialist view with which the reader must be already familiar but the question is most serious - if there are no ways of understanding organisations *objectively*, are there any ways of understanding them *subjectively?* If every individual makes his own interpretation of reality and that is valid for him, how can we understand these differences and discover if they have significance when the individuals are both part of the 'same organisation? It seems almost certain that there is a need to understand organisations if only because the very existence requires responding and coping behaviour. Maybe, for instance, managerial behaviour is not control behavior at all, but rather coping behaviour; the way in which and individual copes with his position in the organisation. In other words, organisational behaviour is the way in which we cope with the world with which others present us. Our perception of the organisation is the framework and conceptual basis which forms the rationale for our behaviour. That is, in order to know what to do we have to define our world and situation in fairly simple and selective terms in order to limit the ways we respond to ways with which we feel; fairly comfortable. For instance. I am deferential towards my boss because that is the way which is most comfortable to me. Infact, he may prefer me to be aggressive but because I cannot risk trying out alternatives I choose the one with which I feel most safe.

In this view, organisations can only be explained in terms of the understanding and perceptions of those who are members and those who are observers. If this brings organisation theory near to any other academic field, it must be the general area of psychology-psychiatry; near to psycho-analysis and psycho-therapy. Both these fields have their problems of scientific credibility but no more so than medicine where definition of illness, disease and health are also problematic not a mention the appropriateness of 'cures' for 'illness'. But at least medicine and psychiatric medicine work as the matching of what the patient believes and what understanding the practitioner is intelligent enough to bring to the situation. A physician who assumes that most complaints are influenza will not always be right; he must have other possibilities in mind including the possibility of the unique syndrome. The advantages of moving away from technical kinds of descriptions of organisations to medical/psychiatric ones lies in the significance of the metaphors we use - since all descriptions or organisations are metaphorical - but also in the openness and caution of the approach. In psychiatry, the practitioner is forced into trying to understand what the patient says; he is also concerned not to categories the condition any more than necessary. It is, for instance, notoriously difficult to get a psychiatrist to define a person as in need of mental certification, but organisation/ management consultants readily assume they can put the organisation to rights. Indeed, the current mood in management thinkings is that all organisations can be improved in some way or another. While it may be true that all organisations can be changed, the desirability of that change must remain a matter of opinion since even on a systems theory basis the long term and ultimate effects of that change cannot be known for some considerable time, if at all.

A phenomenological approach

Intrinsic to the psychiatric, medical psychotherapeutic approaches to observation and deduction is what has come to be termed a phenomenological stance. Since 'phenomenological' looks like being a revived term in management theory and due for over-exposure in the next decade, and since agreement on definition is not yet resolved, we can state here what a phenomenological approach to the study of organisation would mean. At least such a definition made now will enable discussion to centre on the validity of subsequent argument here and will not divert to general semantic debate in another area of concern. The phenomenological view of organisations assumes that each individual makes his own sense of, and gives his own meaning to, the organisations, to which he belongs. Whether an organisation is 'formal' or 'informal' will be a matter of his own interpretation though formal and informal can be taken to be limits in a continuum from high ritual and prescription to low ritual and little prescription. Of course, no-ritual and no-prescription of behaviour would not be organisation. We can define organisation as any situation of human interaction in which patterns of behaviour can be observed. We know of no other definition that is entirely satisfactory.

To understand an organisation from a phenomenological point of view one needs to know what people think about that organisation. Clearly we can never know what *everyone* thinks about it - nor do we ever need to know. If a problem is diagnosed the person who is most significant is the one who defines the problem. Thus, for a manager to say "My workers are lazy," is for him to say "To me, my workers are lazy," and we can only understand the problem of laziness if we understand why the manager believes them to be so. 'Laziness' is his problem, not the workers. The issue here is how we can understand why laziness is a problem to the manager. It is the problem of understanding and interpretation to which we have already referred when discussing research design. Polling workers about their attitude will be of little help since the only question we can ask is, "Do you think you are lazy?" and the answer is likely to be "No." To find out if they are lazy we need production statics but even then we would be assuming that production figures and laziness correlate. Obviously we need a different kind of probing and to do this we need some sort of a hypothesis - but since the situation cannot be a technical one, we cannot use a scientific instrument. We would be better advised to examine how, why and when we make the hypothesis - in other words, to ask why we have such a hunch, to examine our intuition. Most usefully, we might talk to the manager, and to some of the workers and try to make sense of what we hear. This may sound like the third party invention of OD but in a fundamental way it is different because OD relates to an acceptance of the organisation as such being the key element, a "disembodied reality." From a phenomenological stand point organisational significance may or may not be relevant. What the phenomenologist is trying to do is simply to make sense of the situation, not to change it - though he knows it will change.

Is, then, a phenomenological organisation theorist a theorist at all? Is simply anyone entitled to propound organisation theories? Initially, the answer must be yes - since any interpretation must be 'valid' for the interpreter. The onus for understanding is always on the interpreter next in line, and the essential requirements for making valid subjective interpretations are:

1. awareness of one's own value system
2. ability to think logically and abstractly
3. consciously remembered experience of organisations and people's behaviour in them.

The material form in which data about organisations occurs is in some kind of narrative - spoken or written; documentation used within the organisation and outside it but about it; rituals practised in the organisation; projections from individuals in the organisation to those seen to be outside. To make sense of data of this nature an individual requires the sort of training an historian, a literary and dramatic critic, an anthropologist, a psychiatrist might have. Which is a long way from the social-psychology, political economy, operations research training, most organisation theorists appear to have.

Do organisations have objectives or purposes?

A penomenological perspective takes issue with much traditional organisation theory at the point of definition of an organisation. Our definition so far will be totally unacceptable to many people who have a view about organisations, especially economists, political philosophers, financial experts, operations researchers and the general public who think they know what an organisation is. The phenomenologist is not concerned whether in itself an organisation is closely or loosely defined because he takes the definition from the definer. But he also goes further than this because he makes certain 'phenomenological' assumptions or values. Most definitions or organisations assume some sense of objectives or shared objectives, and this is an assumption the phenomenologist cannot share. To the phenomenologist, organisations serve purposes that is, they exist to further the objectives of individuals but they have no objectives themselves. In fact, it is incorrect to speak of objectives since objectives require a conscious defining of activity outcome and evaluation and few, if any, 'objectives' can ever be clearly defined because objectives can only exist in a defined situation and no situation can be properly defined in advance of its arrival. Individuals have hopes, wishes, needs, understandings, values, expectations and all of these are worked out through the organisation of which each is a member; hence organisations serve the purposes of individuals. For this reason no closer definition of an organisation is possible than that they are the experience of individuals who perceive them as organisations of whatever kind.

Because the phenomenological definition of an organisation is particular to itself, most of the other aspects of organisations which other theorists take for granted or as given, are not perceived as having the same significance as is customary. For example, reward is perceived as having meaning only to individuals who perceive and evaluate 'reward' not in terms of what the "organisation" can offer. The idea of collective bargaining and uniform salaries takes on a different meaning if it is seen as part of an individual bargaining process by some members for their own personal satisfaction rather than the seeking of an acceptable reward for all recipients. Furthermore reasons for collective behaviour are seen to be much more complex than many political interpretations give them credit for. The emphasis that a phenomenological approach gives is towards understanding the meaning for individuals of their membership rather than trying to understand the organisation is a technological entity. One the other hand, phenomenology has to take into account the fact that most people *think* of organisations as having a separate and superior existence, that organisations exist in their own right; and that people behave on such premises.

What is organisational structure?

There appear to be three levels at which organisations can be described. The level of individual participation, the level of technical structure, and the level of the organisation as an abstract entity. Most organisation theory has been concerned with technical structure; even the sociological concern with problems of role, leadership, power and authority are essentially structural in concern while all the administrative approaches are overtly structure-conscious. The concern is for better or more effective patterns of communication, improving the use of resources, developing relationships in teams and so forth. Quantitative aspects or organisations are, by their very nature structure-conscious and of course their structure is preoccupied with the technology of the quantitative process not the quantity of the inter-relationships of people. The concept of structure is problematic in organisation theory because though structure is a function of task performance, structures tend to continue beyond the task needs, and to be continued into different tasks, while some theorists appear to believe that there are ideal structures which can be imposed on new situations. A phenomenologist would be unable to prescribe a structure for a situation but would wait for one to emerge. In practice no formal, legally constituted organisation can be set up without a "structure" being put forward but such a structure is notional not real; it is only activated when people begin to interact. The levels at which the organisation actually functions are not the technical level at all but the two other levels of personal involvement and perceived organisational identity. Functioning on the technical level is also personal rather than mechanical. For instance, even in a chemical process plant where the structure appears to be inherent in the process, the levels of individual functioning and organisational perception are human activities not disembodied processes. Individuals cause strikes, stoppages and absences while the ascribed identity to the organisation induces customs to buy the product, consider the firm reliable, to value the training given to operatives and so on.

While it is comparatively straightforward to examine the ways individuals think of the organisation - by using an analytic interview technique, it is more difficult to understand organisation as "entities" We need a basic theory or perspective to describe organisation that is comparable with our theory of people in organisations. If the phenomenological view is that an organisation is what its members perceive or believe it to be then from both inside and outside any organisation is "perceived to be" in some way or another. If we believe a store to a expensive and snobbish, the we shall tend to behave accordingly and may or may not change my opinion whatever my experience. But if the staff at the store perceives that we perceive the store as expensive and snobbish they too will respond accordingly. And if they, for the most part, wish the store to have such an image, so it will stand a good chance of being so perceived by more people. In this way, the collective nature of an organisation consolidates certain dispositions and these dispositions are essentially psychological so that the organisation as an "entity" exists ion a psychological state. There is empirical evidence that organisations have a psychological dimension which is generalised and embracing.

As we mention names of large companies or small shops, a consciousness of the 'image' of that company or shop arises in the mind but the matter goes further than this. Organisations sometimes seem to take on some of the characteristics of individual personality. If we examine churches, some have a 'death wish' and go into decline while others change and adapt. Some organisations behave defensively and aggressively and organisations like the CIA appear to be positively paranoic. Such images probably derive from the characteristics of leading individuals.

The psychology or organisations

It seems logical, that if we look at organisations from a psychological viewpoint, that perspective should apply equally well to examining the organisation as an entity as looking as it as a collection of individuals with varying degrees of sensitivity to the larger organisation. The techniques for understanding organisations by reference to individuals are beginning to come clear; the techniques for understanding organizations in their completeness may well be an extension of the individual methods but are less clear the most useful way of understanding how an individual perceives an organisation is by an unstructured depth interview. The investigator, researcher or consultant talks at length to an individual to find out how the individual sees himself, and how he perceives himself in the organisation. Various interview techniques and approaches are employed deriving from counselling, psychotherapy and encounter group situations. Interviews may also be group interviews, but they are not therapeutic or psychiatric unless the investigator is acting officially as a consultant to the organisation; in this latter case his roll will be to create a helping relationship in an action-research kind of intervention and T - groups, and encounter groups may be used as a means of providing feedback to organisation members themselves. From interviews, a picture of the psychology of the organisation will emerges so that if many individuals feel that the organisation does not value people, some kind of overall view becomes clear which may have implications for the senior staff or boss.

A phenomenological is useful examining the problems that arise from planning. Planning is notoriously unable to account for the unexpected yet the unexpected always happens. Planning is done on the basis of projections based on data, but the selection of data is dependent upon the experience of the planner and his ability to extrapolate from the past. It is impossible to anticipate all eventualities and currently good planning tries to *provide for* the unexpected. The emphasis, however, is more on providing for something that is going to happen, rather than coping with something that has already happened; for example with critical path analysis, PPBS, PERT and so forth. An alternative 'hand to mouth' approach is unacceptable in an industrialised culture: it is seen as the view that 'what will be, will be'. Phenomenology would be more positive. It would recognize the difficulty of knowing all the future, but recognise that in practice much in the future can largely be anticipated and predicted where that future is largely concerned with routine and ritual. However, a phenomenological perspective leads to an emphasis on skills at coping with situations as they happen and creates a functional caution over planning expectation. By adopting a phenomenological stance, the real questions of planning become clearer and can be dealt with in a different way and provision made more carefully for coping with the unexpected.

The validity of subjectivity

There are three areas in which the validity of an organisation theory must be tested—coherence and consistency of the theoretical construct, the applicability of the construct to the situations which it claims to explain, and the devising of relevant research techniques to support the theoretical hypotheses. At the present time, it is in the area of relevant research procedures that there is greatest need. Research approaches are likely to derive from psychotherapy, philosophical analysis, social anthropology, literary criticism rather than the natural and mathematical sciences. Bizarre and eclectic though these sources may seem, they have the advantage of being much concerned, overtly with the question of personal values. Up to this present time the history of social and organisational analysis has been an attempt to prove its scientific credibility but in so doing the wrong techniques have been used. The rational sciences may aim to be vale free—the social sciences cannot avoid values.

7 Management Education and Training Executives

People in business and industry as much as in the Government have asked: What are the conditions for effective management education? How can effectiveness be judged What makes one programme better than another? Some of these problems are examined here and a possible approach to judging effectiveness of the programmes suggested.

Mathematical measurement of the effectiveness of management education is obviously impossible. A company is a complex unit of relationships and at all times a variety of internal and external forces, themselves in a state of flux, influence the situation; it is difficult to isolate from this complex the precise effect of education on the performance of the individual. Yet the very complexity that makes measurement difficult makes it necessary for management to understand the forces which so influence performance. Complexity compels education while it makes difficult the accurate measurement of effectiveness.

Education and training are costly and some

idea of effectiveness and suitability are, therefore, essential for supporting them. Management education expresses its value by determining how a programme can be most effective for participants. It must be conscious of the intrinsic. Problems in this type of education and find solutions for itself before it sets out to be meaningful. In this field, as in many others, there are certain barriers to learning.

Separate fields

A functional distinction between education and training must first be considered. Training prescribes methods of dealing with a given area of activity and the trainer imparts this skill to the participant in a programme.

But management education is primarily concerned with teaching people to think in the presence of new situations. It is the ability to understand the critical influence of internal and external forces bearing upon the activities of an enterprise, and with this knowledge, to choose upon a course of action in full knowledge of its impact on various inter-related aspects of business as well as on the enterprise as a whole.

Training and education as suggested above are not mutually exclusive, but the reason for drawing a distinction is that in the two situations we are really concerned with different problems of learning. Training as stated above is aimed at learning a skill, a prescribed method of application of a technique. These are all specific tasks amenable to precise definition. Education, however, has to deal with more general issues, having to do with the understanding of issues but more so of the participant's own values, his way of looking at the world around him, own beliefs about people and so on. It often means learning not by doing things but by examining ideas which influence the basic components of his personality.

Programmes of education have (a) to create an understanding of the primary influences on situations at work: social, economic, political, technical or legal; (b) analyse the specific situation and determine decision-choices with full knowledge of implications and consequences of each; and (c) ensure personal competence in dealing with problems and situations. This suggests that management education must provide some depth of understanding of the basic forces through the study of disciplines such as psychology, sociology, social anthropology, and economics. Sometimes in this connection a sharp distinction between theory and practice is drawn by some people. This is totally unfounded because both are interdependent and inseparable. The problem is not whether understanding of basic disciplines is necessary but how the material relevant for the manager can be chosen so as to avoid spending more time than necessary on it.

Crux of the problem

I have referred to change as a result of education in the individual's values, his attitudes toward himself, to the group and the society with which he interacts. And I think this, in fact, is the crux of the entire problem. An individual's understanding of research or concepts is guided by what he is willing to accept for himself as being "right." Often, what is right for other people is not seen as being right for oneself; the individual is always the "exception" to the rule. The self image is difficult to disturb and action is satisfactorily rationalised or explained in seemingly logical terms. If management education fails to achieve the objective of "subjective acceptance" of ideas and theory, its achievement is reduced. Management education has, therefore, to consider how subjective understanding or personal involvement of the participant in the process of learning can be achieved. Three issues have to be considered.

First, the desire to learn originates within the individual and cannot be generated by someone outside. That is to say, one cannot really teach others; one can give a discourse, a learned or an interesting one, but this in itself is not enough for people to learn. To this extent a good and learned lecture may create rapport with the listener.

But the participant generally accepts or rejects what the teacher says according to his subjective views. He selects new learning also according to his own biases. This would be truer in some fields than in others but generally to matters that involve the individual himself-his ego, his self. This phenomenon occurs most in respect of social issues where the participant himself is an integral part of the system which he may want to change. He is required to take a view not only from outside as an outsider but from within as a part belonging to the system.

Kurt Lewin, an eminent psychologist in the USA, found in his studies in changing food habits during the war that only when housewives arrived at a conclusion through personal experience did they change their habits. Race relations research or studies by Coch and French Jr. in the industrial setting in changing jobs, etc. have also supported this finding. The point I have made is that learning is optimum when the teacher is to create conditions in which to learn. Conversely, unless the participant has a desire to learn and conditions are created in which he is motivated to learn, learning will not occur.

Inhibiting factors

This problem has much to do with management development efforts in India. Indiscriminate selection of participants for courses inhibits the optimum value of the course. If the participant suspects the motives of this employer in sending him for education or has personal reservations about the course, the use he will make of his time can be discounted.

The administrator-educator sometimes likes to formulate neat looking, water-tight curricula for management courses. This, I think, shows a lack of awareness of learning processes. A rationally based programme by the administrator may be the best reasoned and the most logical one but it has all the unreality of Plato's Republic.

Learning involves self appraisal and one's beliefs and values. It is a function of a number of things such as the teacher-participant relationship, environment, what is taught and how participants are motivated. Often a standard curriculum inhibits a teacher from being able to create suitable conditions for learning and the emphasis of the programme is shifted from learning to its mechanical aspects such as subjects to be covered, examinations and schedules.

The second barrier to learning is that the participant has a preconceived image of himself. New learning is rejected as not being applicable to his own "unique" situation. This often represents the participant's uneasiness to change. He is something like a person abroad who, in the face of the new and the foreign, talks much more about his own culture and the deep roots of his social traditions than he does at home. He is creating an identity for himself. It is not easy to overcome these set images and often it takes a week or two for participants in four-to-six-week programme to stop saying that, really, the boss should have come to the course instead, meaning thereby that the need for new ideas exists for the boss and not for himself.

Thirdly, the belief about a gap between theory and practice is another frequent hurdle that recurs in every educational situation. Often the two are regarded as separate things. This is because theory is misunderstood as being abstract; the participant sometimes fails to realise that theory in fact is derived from experiences often resting on firmer ground than the limited experience of one individual.

Shared experience

Management education must resolve these difficulties in the attempt to be effective; on the removal of these barriers to learning will rest the success of the programmes. A well-thought-out programme must take time and be spread over at least several weeks: residential programmes where the shared experience of one another' side as and the sharing of goals and objectives contribute substantially to resolve these difficulties. Management education does not merely consist of attending a series of lectures given by the academic. Nor is the academic concerned with management education satisfied by merely classroom association with participants. It is for these reasons that duration, the residential nature of the programme and variety in teaching methods become important in management education. Simulation games, the case method, role-playing, sensitivity training, etc, have been used by educators and training officers. There is continuous concern with breaking though the barriers if these methods are employed.

I have argued that a serious evaluation of programmes of education and training is necessary. But because there are no precise, accurate ways of measuring the effectiveness of a particular programme, this must be judged by how well it overcomes barriers to learning. I have pointed out only three barriers which apply to the participant and none in this article which refers to the teaching or scheduling of programmes.

In conclusion, it is necessary that the problems of management education be taken into account in organizing either in company or external programmes of education. Adequate thought is not usually given to these matters. Wasteful control and unwarranted "standardization" of schedules of teaching and curricula should also be cautiously assessed by those concerned with education. Oddly enough, the deliberation of the conferences to which I referred earlier show that there was greater concern with standardization of courses rather than with determining the goals of management education. Successful management in advanced societies requires more than intuitive judgement and luck, though both these are important and have played a spectacular role in their sphere of activity. We believe that in the next ten years or so this would be increasingly true for India as well. Experience alone, or shrewd intuitiveness by itself, would be insufficient. This will be more true of management of industries that are science-and-technology based, such as chemicals, electronics, machine tools and several others.

Although intuition in management tasks is relevant, it cannot be taught. Hence, a majority of people and many managers will be required to rely on systematic ways of managing business. They will be required to use related and reliable data to perform their tasks. To face up to this requirement other than intuitive skills would be needed. Some of the skills are: developing appropriate organisational systems, those skills that can deal with analysis, collation and interpretation of usable data, and using these for better decision purposes. Equally important would be the human skills that minimise the strain and anxiety of employees in tasks that are new and demanding as well as frequently changing.

Evidence from the industrial societies, and from the Indian experience, already shows that management tasks do make these various demands and suggests a future where they will be ever more pressing. I think it is in this context that we need to look at the training of executives. The onus of helping the transition rests both with the organisations and the instructors; for creating the conditions in which training would be most effective, and providing such instruction as is totally meaningful for the maturation of the manager's task.

The most reliable criterion of success of a programme of training is overall improvement in the manager's performance. There are companies that have benefited from training and those that have not. The success or failure of training is not accidental. I think there are differences in the number of ways in which training is made use of; and these, perhaps, make the differences between success and failure. When one has had the advantage of observing this difference both as an executive and as a teacher, it becomes necessary to brush aside wishful thinking and explanations or excuses and look constructively at management training as we teach and imbibe it.

For me the most difficult discipline as a teacher has been to set aside the temptation to impose my own interests on the participants and, instead, to seek out the participants' interests on which to base my instruction. I believe a choice of this nature does not confront only the teaching profession but almost all other walks of life; among peers, as well as in the relationship of 'superior" and "subordinate", father and son, supervisor and worker, manager and staff. Nor is this choice absent in the relationship between trainer and trainee in a management training programme. Rarely, very rarely indeed, does he consider, and work upon, the participant's personal goals, or the particular circumstances of the trainee in his situation of work.

It is not unnatural that his paradox exists in training programmes. The instructor expects the participant to mould himself according to the instructor's anticipations. The individual's personal goals seldom come into the vortex of learning. Can this be a reason for the fact that sending managers to training courses or setting up in-company training facilities by themselves do not improve performance?

One chief executive stated that approximately 60 per cent of the junior and middle level executives had attended his company's executive programmes or those organised by outside groups, but it was hard to see any change in their performance. This is understandable. Could it be, then, that for training to be effective, the organisation has to provide conditions that enable employees to use their training with benefit to their work performance?

In this paper I wish to suggest conditions that may account for poor returns on training expenditures and later I will suggest some possible aims that trainers could try to achieve in their programmes.

In evaluating such matters perhaps we need to avoid wishful generalisations and beliefs that a device, without conducive conditions, can by itself cause noticeable change for the better. Unless management *manages* effectively, none of the other activities is likely to have the desired impact. Given *a competent* system of management, executive training or other aids can provide the most powerful support that management could have. It seem to me that we can formulate a golden rule for incurring massive costs on training on the following lines:

If the chief executives and his aides feel that they themselves need to change in some ways and, therefore desire to work toward change even at the cost of the inevitable personal pain inherent in any changed situation, the organisation is likely to receive full value for executive training.

The top management's unwillingness to change themselves conveys two meanings to others. One, that only at lower levels are employees inadequate and therefore need a *brain-*

washing exercise and this, of course, is resented; two, that change can be achieved at lower levels without change at top levels. The truth is that change is resisted in the board room as much as on the factory floor. Contradictions of this kind seriously diffuse the impact of training and minimise the use executives make of it.

There are three issues inherent in training that require to be often restated. They are, that training:

(a) is useful for *some* and not for *all*,

(b) can serve *some* purposes but not *all* purposes, and

(c) is useful provided the firm is capable of using it

These points require to be explained further:

(a) No one learns in a classroom or on his job unless he *really* has the urge to learn. A teacher can, at most, make the subject interesting, but if the executive sees no personal gain in learning the subject, it is unlikely that even the best teacher can help him much. I have personally found the difference between participants who came because they wanted to come and those who were served a notice by the boss to attend a programme. Admittedly some persons are even nominated for reasons other than to enable the participant to obtain education or learning. Some common reasons are: to get to know people from other companies; or to have a paid holiday for good work done; or because other companies send their executives. I believe, however, that if a company wants to nominate someone for a course, and the nominators want to use this training to their best advantage, some choice between attending and not attending the course should be given to the participant.

(b) Education can provide what the name suggests. The better institutions, which are interested in experimentation with teaching methods and with diffusion of learning at conscious level, will help the participant to face up to the problem of using the knowledge he has gathered. But education cannot make him a better person than he is. In a recent course for general management I met a participant who was sent there because his manager thought that he was inadequate in developing interpersonal relationships. For most of the course the individual concerned sat alone and looked wistfully at the others who ignored him. If the purpose of sending him was to improve his interpersonal relations the course was not best suited for the individual concerned. he should have been sent to our laboratory programme or one primary concerned with such issues.

The misfit situation arises in other ways as well. For example, the individual may be promoted to a job far above his capacity. The superior hopes that training might do wonders for him and that a few weeks' contact with the trainers or other participants may supply the needed capability. It is unlikely that raining can make up for poor selection. This mistake could be corrected not by nominating the individual to a course, but by administrative action. Training may draw out the trainee's hidden capabilities but cannot induce a quality that is not in his make-up.

(c) Assuming that both these aspects are satisfactory, the training will be meaningful only if the individual's superior has the ability to use this new learning on the participant's return. If an organisation is rigid in its systems and procedures and permits little scope for experimentation with new ideas, the participants will be too scared to use his learning without conscious and specify encouragement by the superior. Under these conditions a *fade-out* occurs. What has been learnt, but not used, quickly passes out of his memory. Some illustrations from my personal experience would be relevant here.

(i) A works manager of a large plant was greatly involved in learning during a management course, and he worked very hard. On his return he mildly suggested to his superior a change in certain established practices. His suggestions were received with such stern disapproval that he gave up all effort to make use of whatever he had a painstakingly learnt.

(ii) After an intensive three month programme, a junior executive tried to keep his section

isolated from the *political systems* in the company, but meeting with constant sneers from colleagues and little support from higher executives, he gave up, and became fully involved in the power game in his company.

(iii) In another organisation the participant was able to use his learning to advantage. The head of a large department began to use his new learning with the support of his general manager and found that, in course of time, his subordinates and some of the other departments had begun to change their practices. This resulted in greater cooperative activities in the company as a whole.

(iv) There is a consistent expression of the view that the course would be most suitable for the *bosses* of those who attended the course. Underlying this expression is the *well-founded* feeling that without the boss changing his ways, there is little chance that the participant can change.

Briefly I like to advance the following three propositions:

1. If the chief executive and senior managers are unwilling themselves to go for training, it is unlikely that their subordinates would be enthusiastic to go, and even if they are, they would benefit little from it.

2. If the company is not used to self-questioning and experimentation, it is unlikely that the participant will use his learning to sufficient advantage.

3. If the person is not capable of learning, or has no choice but to go to a programme, he is unlikely to make the best use of the facilities open to him.

All training has to do with improvement of the individual his job-related knowledge and his interpersonal skills. Given an appropriate task system, the executive's ability as a decision-maker, or as a manager, would be enhanced. I believe that serious training activity which excludes either one aspect or the other is inadequate. Training must naturally expect that the executive would do things differently, after training, from what he did before. This change entails undergoing the painful experience of first admitting to himself that his ways may not always have been the most adequate and secondly, gaining confidence in himself and his work environment to risk experimentation and a possible failure. He has to develop an intellectual understanding of the subject matter as well as adjust to the emotional acceptance of strange, new ideas. For this to happen, the individual has to be personally "involved" in the learning process. Most schools of management education have been constantly looking for a pedagogy of a kind that would serve these needs. Let me illustrate this by example of two separate courses which aim at integrating subject knowledge and interpersonal relationship by optimum involvement of the participant.

One example is of a seven-day programmes whose objective was to understand how organizations develop task systems and role relationships, patterns of authority, power and control, and similar organisational processes. There were no lectures in this programme. The participants had to learn from the experience they themselves generated and from the problems set for them by the instructors. By the design of the programme, the participants gained insight into their own behaviour, their relationships with others and organisational processes. We believe that in a short space of one week participants learnt more in this kind of programme than they do in courses of longer duration.

Another example is that of a course for second-year students at out Institute. It is scheduled for three days in a week for a term of twelve weeks. The primary objective of the course is to examine how a manager manages to maintain a high level of achievement among the members under his command. There are theoretical as well as experience-oriented issues into which he must gain insight. But one without the other is not sufficient. A typical week's schedule runs as follows: first day, discussion on theory and concepts; next day, working on tasks in small groups to identify organisational processes; and the third day, making a presentation of one of the managerial tasks. The onus of learning is mainly on the student and he is personally involved in the process of learning.

I am sure there are other pedagogical devices that are useful and effective. The principal object of the design and its pedagogy should be to achieve such an integration. For me, executive training does not consist of a series of lecturers on a list of topics. They are useful, indeed, but by themselves they do not provide *complete* education to a trainee in the pursuit of self-growth.

8 Management and Morale

Concerning the practice of some social scientists

In the preceding chapter we have been concerned with theories which fail to represent cooperative phenomena as the executive intuitively experiences them. This criticism cannot be made of all generalizations in the field of social science. Some of them have been developed in relation to practice and in a context comparable to that of the administrator. The clinician, whether he be psychiatrist, psychologist, psychopathologist, psychoanalyst, or child psychologist, when he has been concerned with helping people to adjust more effectively to t their environment, has had to deal with the theorize about cooperative phenomena in a position of responsibility. The sociologist, the social anthropologist in his field investigations of communities, the social case worker, the penologist have been in similar positions.

From them a great deal of empirical knowledge has been gained. Among them exists a common fund of knowledge acquired from dealing with essentially the same class of phenomena; and yet, curiously enough, this common knowledge has remained, just as we did in the case of the administrator, the skillful clinician who does a good job with little theory and sometimes even in spite of the theories he holds. We also find those who can expound with great ease and clarity the theories of Freud and yet would be stumped if presented with a concrete case of psychoneurosis to handle.

It is our opinion that this common element underlying the practice of these different specializations has been only too evident. Only those whose orientation to words and labels is so strong as to make the orientation to situations impossible could fail to see, for example, the similarity in context which exists in certain important respects for the administrator handling a dissatisfied employee, for the psychiatrist handling a mild case of obsession, or for the social worker handling a client. Granted that there are also important differences among these three situations which should be kept in mind, there are certain simple generalizations which apply to the effective handling of all of them.

It seems absurd to think that in dealing with such common phenomena the administrator should think about the human being in one way, the psychiatrist in another way, and the social worker in still another—that each should have different theories with regard to human motivation and behavior. There is no wide and sharp split of orientation between the practice of the garage mechanic and the practice of the engineer or the physicist. We do not find garage mechanics trying to exorcise devils out of the hoods of automobiles—a class of phenomena with which the physicist or engineer is not concerned. Why then should there be this sharp and wide split of orientation between the administrator, the psychiatrist, and the sociologist, when each is dealing with essentially the same limited class of phenomena? If in fact it does not exist in skillful practice, why does it exist in theory?

It will be the purpose, therefore, of this chapter to make a few simple statements with regard to what seems to us to be the general common orientation in point of view and method which exists among all these different specializations, when it comes down to the responsible practice of them in dealing with that limited class of phenomena we have called "cooperative." In our opinion, the essential groundwork of collecting facts and the systematic search for simple uniformities among them in a wide variety of situations have not as yet gone very far. A few simple steps have been taken in this direction, and each step has more than confirmed our expectations; but more research is needed. What is said here can be only tentative and suggestive. As we have said before, our hope is to stimulate more research and less talk about matters of human collaboration. To talk very much about a knowledge which exists, if at all, in only an embryonic stage puts one into an uncomfortable position. We shall try to set a good example by being brief.

Concerning the control of cooperative phenomena

Probably the simplest statement we have made, perhaps only by suggestion, is that practice occurs in the present and not in the future. We cannot practice in the future; we can only practice *here and now*. If, therefore, we are to control future events, particularly events involving the interactions of persons, we must do something here and now which will have the desired consequences. When effective control is to be exercised by the executive, it has to be exercised at the point of action in the present.

Therefore, the kind of knowledge which tells an executive what a desirable state of affairs in his human organization should be is not so helpful as statements regarding the immediate steps he should take in order to reach this end. It is one thing to tell him that the "morale" of his organization is not very high; it is another thing to know what to do here and now in order to improve it.

We have met this problem before. A person's performance can be measured in terms of a standard. But in what sense is his behavior controlled? The standard can tell how much a person's performance falls short of what is expected of him; it may determine whether or not a person is allowed to stay on the job. This is one kind of "control" which the executive can exercise. Under certain conditions the standard may control the person's future performance; that is, his performance may improve. This is another kind of "control." But whether it improves or not, the standard says absolutely nothing with regard to why here and now the person's performance falls short of what is expected of him and what can be done here and now to improve it. This is a third kind of "control."

This last kind of control can be exercised only through a diagnosis of the human situation. It depends upon a diagnosis of the present factors limiting the person's performance. It means operating here and now upon these limiting factors. When an administrator is in this orientation, he is acting very much like a physician or an engineer, although he is dealing with another class of phenomena. He is exercising "human control" by a knowledge of the uniformities among relations existing in the situation here and now, and he is acting here and now in terms of these uniformities.

There is another type of human control the executive can exercise which in some respects may be very similar, but in other respects very different. Any person who is in a position of responsibility in a business organization may exercise human control by using words or stimuli of one kind or another to impose certain standards of behavior. In this way he hopes to bring about certain future events. Much of our language has this function—through words we attempt to direct, influence, control the future actions of our fellow men.

Generally the language we use for this purpose is anything but matter of fact; it is likely to be full of feeling and emotion. Perhaps it is for this reason that we fail to note that the "standards" in terms of which we measure the performance of a person may have exactly the same function. They are "controls" only in the sense that they influence the future action of people by imposing patterns of behavior. In this sense, the difference between the old-fashioned supervisor who exercised control by saying, "Bill, get the lead out of your pants," and the modern supervisor who exercises control by pointing out to Bill his performance in relation to a standard is only one of degree. To the extent that the old-fashioned supervisor may have known Bill and his situation and addressed his remark to that context, while the modern supervisor may be addressing his standard to an undifferentiated worker, the former may have an edge on the latter. In either case, the explicit understanding of the human situation is lacking.

This example may help to distinguish the two different kinds of control. In one case we may try to influence a person's behavior by using words which are addressed to that person's situation. We hope that they will have the desired effect because they are utterances with collective sanction in the group of which the person is a member, or they are appealing to that person's most fundamental residues of behavior. In the other case we may use the same words without effect because they are not being addressed to that particular situation. The first kind of control, if done either explicitly or intuitively, does not differ very much from the kind of control we previously mentioned—a control which is dependent upon a knowledge of the uniformities among relations existing here and now in the situation. The second kind of control is quite different. It becomes a sort of verbal magic—a kind of control which has long since disappeared in the exact sciences—an attempt to control future events by magical words rather than by an understanding of situations.

In the case of our previous example, the supervisor who says to Bill, "Get the lead out of your pants," with a explicit knowledge of or at least an acquaintance with Bill and his situation and the collective sentiments and beliefs of the group of which Bill is a member, may be acting very effectively. Without such knowledge, however, the hope that in all cases all workers can be motivated by the phrase, "Get the lead out of your pants," is futile. The same point can be made about standards. Standards, too, can constitute effective human control or can be nothing more than exercises in verbal magic. Whether they are one or the other depends upon the way they are being used and a knowledge of the situation to which they are being applied. But how is this knowledge of human situations acquired?

What "psychopathologists" have had to say about the control of cooperative phenomena

Modern psychopathology has contributed a great deal to the subject of "control." According to this school of thought, man has roughly two ways of controlling his environment: (1) by trying to change his environment to conform to his wishes, and (2) by modifying his wishes and expectations to fit in with his environment. Whichever form this control takes in a particular situation, the better part of wisdom is to control those things over which one can have some control and not to try to control those things over which one can have little or no control. For example, if a person is worried about what his fellow associates think of him, it is sometimes better for him to try to control his preoccupation that he is not liked by his fellow associates—something over which he can learn to exercise some control—rather than to go around frantically trying to get his fellow associates to like him, that is, trying to control the likes and dislikes of other people—something over which he has no control. On the other hand, if a person is afraid of being run over by a train and he happens to be standing on a railroad track and hears a train approaching, it is wiser for him to control the situation by jumping off the track than to try to control his fear.

"Control" in this sense implies knowing something about the class of phenomena to which the control is to be applied in a given situation. Psychopathology has shown that people who have difficulty in getting along with their fellow men, or who, for one reason or another, are nervous, harassed, timid, or apprehensive, can be helped by a minute exploration of their situations in order to determine those factors here and now which are tending to produce these symptoms and difficulties. In this connection it should be remembered that many things which happened years ago can operate here and now in the form of interfering preoccupations.

Now this implies a new conception of human control. It implies a control through an understanding of situations. By such understanding a person can gradually find out what he needs to do as well as what he can do here and now to make matters better for himself. He may, for example, learn that he should seek more the association of other people and learn how to live and work better with his fellow men. He may try to do something in this direction and painfully and slowly acquire new social skills of relating himself to his fellow men—skills with which his early family situation and later educational development had failed to provide him. He may find, at the same time, that he also needs to change certain maps inside his head which are inaccurately representing the kind of world in which he lives. This is another class of phenomena. He may find that some of his trouble comes from the fact that he is trying to make the world conform to these peculiar maps inside his head rather than trying to make these maps conform to the kind of world in which he lives. In this process of acquiring insight, his expectations may become modified. Instead of asking the world to conform entirely to his wishes, he learns how to relate himself to the world in which he lives. Between these two tendencies, he learns to achieve a comfortable working equilibrium.

Now many people who are skillfully helping others in this fashion—regardless of the labels they may bear, the different ways in which they may state the techniques they practice, and the different theories they may profess—are expressing in practice a very similar orientation. It is an orientation which addresses itself to the concrete situation. The control they exercise is achieved through understanding how a person got that way before recommending a cure. It pays attention to limiting conditions as well as to the strategic factors in the present situation about which something can be done. In many cases of personal maladjustment, the structure of the thinking here and now may be the most important factor; and it is often the thing about which something not only should be but can be done.

What "sociologists" and "social anthropologists" have had to say about the control of cooperative phenomena

Sociologists and social anthropologists have also thrown considerable illumination on the problem of control. According to this school of thought, man from the date of birth lives in a social milieu. This social milieu is not a mere aggregate of individuals; it is ordered set of conditions which has a character. In short, man is born into a specific family group which has certain ways of life, certain codes of behaviour. It is related in certain ways to other families in the community. It has a certain cultural background. The process of educating the new member who is born into a specific family group is to transmit the existing culture to him. It is preparing him for social life—

for increasingly wider social participation. In this process not only the immediate family group, but the school and the church also play their parts. The early meanings a person assigns to his experience are largely in terms of these codes of behavior and associated beliefs. As the child grows up and participates in groups other than the immediate family, he loses more and more of his egocentricity. He learns to achieve more adequate social skills of relating himself to his social environment.

This point of view suggests that these cultural patterns of behavior, this vast network of customary ways of doing things into which we are born, constitute the chief control on our lives. Only by such codes is behavior predictable or cooperation possible. Only through them can social control be exercised. Without them there would be no such thing as society. In order to exist, society must impose patterns of behavior on its members. It must make husbands dutiful to their wives,children obedient to their parents.

Now any administrator or person responsible for the work of others intuitively recognizes that much effective collaboration among people is dependent upon conforming to certain codes of behavior without any conscious process of deciding whether one will or will not cooperate. A standard with collective sanction for the group to which it is applied is easier to administer than a standard without such sanction, for without such sanction the standard can be maintained only by force.

Without accepted codes of behavior the spontaneity of collaboration is lost. Although this is intuitively understood by the skillful practitioner of human relations, it is far from being explicitly recognized in the partial logics of management by means of which "control" is also exercised.

Concerning a useful way of thinking about cooperative phenomena

Our point up to now has been that effective human control can be exercised by a person in a position of responsibility only through a adequate understanding of the human situations he is administering. He has to know something about the individuals under his charge; he has to know something about their social as well as technical organization. He has to be alert to changes which may be occurring in either or both of these areas and their possible effects on the total situation; for example, what effects in his organization may result from a rapid introduction of new employees or of new techniques. All this requires a capacity on his part to diagnose the individual and group situations under his charge. For this purpose he use certain intuitive skills. But can these skills be more clearly formulated?

If these skills are capable of being made explicit and of being taught, they involve, as we have stated before: (1) a clear understanding of the limited class of phenomena to which they are addressed, (2) a useful way of thinking about this class of phenomena, and (3) simple methods for obtaining the data. We have had much to say about understanding the limited class of phenomena with which these skills are concerned. We have tried to demonstrate that cooperative phenomena are capable of being clearly differentiated from other classes of phenomena and of constituting a legitimate field of inquiry. We shall now consider the other two requirements.

Concerning a useful way of thinking about cooperative phenomena

By indirection, we have been suggesting a concept of equilibrium as a useful way of regarding the complex interactions of people in a cooperative system. It is a way of thinking which, if followed, prevents us from making a simple cause-and-effect analysis of phenomena in which a relation of inter-dependence obtains. We have been suggesting the concept of a social system in which the components of the system are individuals having certain properties as well as certain relations to one another. "The properties and relations of persons exist not in a changeless state, but in a state of flux. However, the instantaneous states and the changes are not chaotic or random states and changes. On the contrary, they are in general subject to connections and constraints of a kind that may be referred to, or considered as in a measure determined by, the condition of equilibrium...defined by Pareto as 'a state such that if a small modification different from that which will otherwise occur is impressed upon a system, a reaction will at once appear tending toward the conditions that would have existed if the modification had not been impressed.'"

In Part I, we have been giving popular expression to this point of view. We have been suggesting that in a business organization some of the important properties and relations of the components of the system are:

(1) the "social conditioning" of the individuals who go to make up the organization—what they are bringing to the situation in terms of (a) social codes of behavior, collective beliefs, and sentiments, (b) personal skills, (c) a social attitudes—obsessive and irrational preoccupations, (d) economic interests, and (e) logical skills;

(2) the formal patterns of behavior of the organization, with their associated sentiments and beliefs, to which the individual has to conform and which are prescribed by the rules, regulations, and policies of the company—which we shall generally refer to as "formal organization";

(3) the informal patterns of behavior of particular work groups, with their associated sentiments and beliefs, to which the individual also has to conform, i.e. the particular codes and routines of behavior of local groups—which we shall refer to as "informal organization."

We can conceive of these parts as so interrelated and inter dependent that any change in one part of the social system will be accompanied by changes in other parts of the system. There is a disparity in the rates of change possible in different parts of the system. The formal organization can change more rapidly than the informal; the informal organization can change more rapidly than the social conditioning of the individuals who go to make up informal work groups.In this disparity in the rates of change we shall look for conditions of unbalance which may manifest themselves in different forms.

It is our contention that this condition of equilibrium is that to which the skillful administrator is addressing himself when handling cooperative phenomena. It is through his understanding of this condition of equilibrium, and the possible sources of interference which may produce an unbalance, that be exercises "control." It is only through his knowledge of the factors making for or against the condition of equilibrium that he can do something here and now. It is a control of the future by an understanding of the conditions determining the present state of equilibrium rather than an attempt to produce future event B by putting into effect event A with the hope that cause A will produce effect B regardless of the situation of equilibrium that obtains.

This is the administrative context in which men of action who are responsible for the actions of others often find themselves. From the point of view of the nervous system it is not a comfortable position in which to be. It is often difficult to produce a desirable state of affairs B under the present conditions of equilibrium A, for the factors determining equilibrium A may be such as to allow B to be achieved only by introducing undesirable factors C, D, and E. It is little wonder that men who daily live in this context are often rendered speechless and feel they are misunderstood by social reformers, social planners, and social theorists. Dreams of Utopia have little place in their lives. It is their function to keep the world steady for others, that is, to maintain that condition of equilibrium which makes for feelings of security and "morale" in their organizations.

Concerning simple methods of obtaining the data

Both psychopathology and sociology have contributed useful method to the study and diagnosis of individual and group situations. One may be called "the interviewing method"; the other may be called "the method of social observation." Through the combined use of both methods, in any human situation in a business organization one can learn what is important to people—their hopes and fears, what may be the sources of their dissatisfactions and difficulties, to what groups they belong, the extent and nature of their participation, their positions in informal groups, as well as the effect that technical changes, management logics, and methods of supervision may have on these factors. As a result, a human diagnosis of the concrete situation can be made in terms of which something can be done here and now, if need be, to improve the cooperative situation.

It may be well here to consider the extent to which the administrator himself should or can practice these skills of diagnosing human situations. Although from a certain aspect this is an important consideration, we have not dealt with this problem anywhere in this book. Our position is very simple and brief. It seems to us of first importance, at this stage of our development, to state the conditions and limits of the skills, the limited class of phenomena to which they can be applied and practiced usefully under certain given conditions. This has been the level at which this book has been written. It has been affirming two propositions: (1) these skills can be clearly formulated, can be made communicable, and can be usefully applied; (2) business organizations, particularly large ones, need them. It therefore seemed of secondary importance to try to state how these skills can or should be introduced in a business organization and by whom they should be applied—by the line administrator or a staff specialist. In fact, to say anything on this matter is either taking out of turn and trying to control things over which we have no control, or trying to dictate to whom knowledge should be made available.

In terms of the limited experience we have had so far, it is our opinion that these skills can be practiced at different levels. It seems to us common sense that there should be no cleavage in orientation or point of view with regard to thinking about cooperative phenomena among the different people in positions of responsibility in a business organization who deal with such phenomena. But with the systematic daily application of these skills to concrete situations, a number of peculiar considerations come in which will vary from one organization to an other. It is perhaps needless to say that these skills cannot be learned overnight and that they have to be practiced in order that persons should become proficient in their use.

Management and morale

It may be surprising to some that the word "morale" has appeared so infrequently in a chapter on the subject. This has been done intentionally to avoid thinking about a vague word. Rather, the intention has been to think about more concrete phenomena to which, if it is to have any meaning, the word "morale" can now be referred.

For any person who has held a position of responsibility in a business organization—or any organization for that matter—the word "morale" comes to have real meaning; that is, it refers to something which is felt to be of great importance, even if that something remains vague and illusive. It pertains to the relations of individuals in a group or larger organization, rather than to the individual alone. To talk of the "morale" of an individual, apart from the group or organization to which he contributes his services, is to talk about personal characteristics of behavior outside of cooperative systems. Individuals can be so characterized. It will be remembered that we did mention certain individuals who because of their past social experiences were unfitted for cooperation. In this sense it is well to remember that the social conditioning of the individuals who make up an organization may constitute an important factor in determining the character of the cooperation or "morale," particularly if the individuals have not been well prepared for cooperation and need assistance in making an adjustment.

Like many such words, the word "morale" jumps into prominence when that to which it refers is either conspicuously absent or conspicuously present. Like the state of our health, it be comes most important when we lose it. "Morale," in its everyday manifestations, is likely to be ignored and disregarded. Many aspects of our everyday existence have this character; that is, they include factors which we take for granted and whose important functions we therefore fail to recognize until they are drastically changed or disappear. We mentioned this point in connection with our discussion of routine ways of behaving which bind us in collaborate effort. Only when we lose a customary way of doing things, only when we are threatened with the loss of our customary way of life, do we realize its importance to us. Nothing makes us feel more insecure, uncertain, apprehensive, and demoralized than to have our routine ways of behavior too quickly and too arbitrarily interfered with.

The primitive assumes that all is well if he preserves his traditional ways of doing things; the economic problems will more or less take care of themselves. Modern man assumes that all is well if the technical and economic factors determining the production and distribution of goods are taken care of; the social codes of human association will more or less take care of themselves. And then, perhaps indulging somewhat in oversimplification, we concluded, "As a result we have the goods, but the natives have the morale."

Let us continue with the analogy between health and morale. In medicine, for example, the physician is not interested in health or sickness in general; he is interested in diagnosing and treating particular organic situations. He has no treatment of disease in general; his treatment follows rather than precedes diagnosis; it is specific to the diagnosis of the particular organic ailment and the personal situation of the patient. Why then should we think that because there is a word "morale" there is one thing to which it refers? Why then should we think that we can treat something in general before we know in particular the many different states and kinds of equilibrium—personal and social—to which this word may refer? In medicine such an attitude has long since disappeared. To those who still think that certain herbs can cure all illnesses, a certain unafavorable label is now applied. But there are many of us who still think that certain magical words, regardless of the particular situations to which they are applied, can produce morale. It may be well to remember that to people who have lost their traditional ways of work, who are living in a social void, these symbols may have lost their customary significance. They may cease to motivate, except in a direction we do not want.

Although the physician has no specific remedies for sickness in general, he does have a simple and useful way of thinking about the physical organism. He conceives of the organism as being made up of parts which are interrelated and interdependent. That is, he conceives of the physical organism in relation to its physical environments as a physicochemical system—something which must be considered as a whole because each part bears a relation of interdependence to every other part. These parts are in a relation of equilibrium such that a slight change in one part produces changes in other parts of the system tending toward restoring the equilibrium. In this sense he does conceive of ill health or sickness as an organic unbalance of some kind; but the nature of the particular unbalance, the particular interferences making for unbalance, and hence the particular treatment required to restore the balance, can be determined only by a study of the concrete case of the particular patient. And this is where the skill and experience of the physician come in. As a result, the treatment, far from being the same, is different for different patients even though the symptoms may be very similar. In the case of patient A, this point of view leads to a diagnosis which prescribes treatment A; in the case of patient B, it leads to a diagnosis which prescribes treatment B.

It is our thesis that what physical health is to a physical organism, morale is to a cooperative system. Lack of morale, like lack of health, cannot often be reduced to some one simple cause. Just as problems relating to health require a simple and useful way of thinking about the physical organism as a physicochemical system, so an understanding of problems relating to morale requires a simple and useful way of thinking about human beings in their associations with one another as a social system.

From this point of view, the problems of morale in a business organization break down into two parts: (1) the daily problems of maintaining internal equilibrium within the organization, that is, maintaining that kind of social organization in which individuals and groups through working together can obtain human satisfactions that will make them willing to contribute their services to the economic objective of cooperation; and (2) the daily problems of diagnosing possible sources of interference, of locating sore spots, of liquidating human tensions and strains among individuals and groups, of helping people to orient themselves to their work groups, of spotting blockages in the channels of communication. These are the two "human controls" exercised by the administrator.

Maintaining internal equilibrium within the social organization of the plant involves keeping the channels of communication free and clear so that orders are transmitted downward without distortion and so that relevant information regarding situations at the work level is transmitted upward without distortion to those levels at which it can be best made use of. This involves getting the bottom of the organization to understand the economic objectives of the top; it also means getting the top of the organization to understand the feelings and sentiments of the bottom. It involves moving people about in the organization—transferring, upgrading, downgrading, promoting, demoting, placing, and selecting—in a manner that will be in accordance with the social values of the human situation and hence in a manner that will preserve morale.

This is the problem of morale in its everyday manifestation. In this context morale is not a quality attaching to an individual or to a group; it is a dynamic relation of equilibrium between individuals and the organization they serve. To call the word "morale" into being when cooperation has ceased to exist in fact is too late. It should also be noted that in this context the administrator is the guardian or preserver of morale through the function of maintaining a condition of equilibrium which will preserve the social values existing in the cooperative system. Only in this sense does he have "authority."

To preserve the social values existing in the cooperative system, the administrator needs skills of diagnosing human situations. To expect him to exercise effective control, to maintain authority, to obtain loyalty and confidence without such skills is to ask him to stay in a horse-and-buggy stage with regard to this aspect of his job when the remainder of it has long since become streamlined. It is our contention that these skills no longer need to remain intuitive and personal. They can be clearly formulated and applied. The introduction of these skills in our modern business organizations is the challenge of our times. There is a need for the explicit recognition and systematic application of a specialty which is addressing itself to the adequate diagnosis and understanding of the actual human situations—both individual and group—within the business organization. This is the intelligent exercising of control. It is addressing ourselves to concrete situations and finding out what are present here and now in the form of interferences and what can be done here and now to correct them.

This job needs to be done continuously, even daily. To expect that human problems can be fixed up once and for all is absurd. No matter how well they are handled, local unbalances will arise. They need to be continuously attended to. To expect loyalty and confidence and willingness to contribute their services from people whose feelings of personal integrity have been damaged—no matter how unwittingly—is to ask for the moon.

It is our hope that in time, through the practice of these skills, the word "morale" will drop from the vocabulary of administrators and their staff specialists concerned with human situations, just as the word "health" has dropped from the terminology of medicine. In its place will be substituted effective classification of human situations and skillful methods of treating them. In this modern organization it will become just as old-fashioned to ask, "What is the state of morale of your department?" as for a physician to go into a modern hospital and ask, "what is the state of health of our patients?" In its place will be asked, "What are the particular human situations in your department, and how are you handling them?" This will be the exercise of "control" by understanding and not by ritualistic, verbal practices which address themselves to human nature in general, but not to *particular* human beings in *particular* places with particular feelings and sentiments for which they need concrete social expression.

9 Paradigm Diversity in Organizational Research

Introduction

In recent years, increasing attention has been devoted to understanding how the assumptions which scientists bring to their subject of investigation guide and influence what is seen and studied. In the field of organization studies, the problems involved have been most systematically explored through the notion of 'paradigm', and many rival modes of analysis identified and offered as alternative frameworks for the study of organization. The demonstrated existence of diversity, and more importantly the possibility of increased diversity in the future, poses organizational scientists with a situation that can be interpreted either as threat, opportunity, or some combination thereof.

Paradigm diversity is most often interpreted as threat by those organizational scientists committed to well-established models and methods for understanding organizations, and who wish to understand the generation of knowledge as a gradual, cumulative, well-ordered process. Paradigm diversity from their point of view is often seen as challenging the legitimacy of what they feel they already know about organization, and as opening a 'Pandora's box' of new problems and issues that must be addressed. For example, new paradigms entail new modes of theoretical conceptualization, the use of different research tools and techniques, and an appeal to new criteria for determining the legitimacy and quality of the knowledge which they generate. In essence, the perception of paradigm diversity as threat hinges on a celebration of past achievement and a fear and concern that a free and open pursuit of new directions will challenge and undermine this achievement.

The interpretation of diversity as opportunity, on the other hand,celebrates the possibility of obtaining new insights and understanding. Established paradigms for theorizing and research are recognized as providing at best partial modes of understanding which may be supplemented or even replaced by those of new paradigms. The constructive, perhaps cautious, opportunist seeks to emphasize the possibilities and advantages of exploring the new. The more dogmatic opportunist seeks to replace on orthodoxy with another, emphasizing the supremacy of one or more competing paradigms over the others. Either way, the challenge of diversity is seen as resting in the potential it offers for developing new modes of understanding the phenomenon of organization.

The paradigms discussed by Burrel and Morgan are not merely typologies, and the primary purpose of conceiving social theory and organizational analysis in these terms is not simply to classify theory and research in terms of different dimensions and to determine the location of one social or organizational theorist *vis-a-vis* another. The paradigms and the dimensions through which they are characterized present the interested social scientist with an invitation to discern and explore the deep structure of assumptions which underlie different modes of theorizing. Theorizing characteristic of the different paradigms constructs the social world in very different ways, and leads us to see and understand the nature of organization in different ways. The fundamental challenge posed by a recognition of this paradigm diversity is to see and understand how we can research organization in ways that tell us something new about the phenomenon in which we are interested. This challenge also leads to others, explores elsewhere, such as the need to reconcile the form, legitimacy and claims of one mode of knowledge against another, by reflecting on the way organizational researchers attempt to understand their subject of investigation.

We can begin to see the prospects and possibilities which the different paradigms offer organizational analysis by posting the question, 'What does each paradigm contribute to our understanding of organization?' In the following four sections of this chapter, I attempt to answer this question by adopting the different perspectives which characterize each paradigm, identifying just four or five of the major contributions which each has to offer. In the final section of the chapter, identify some of the issues that needs to be addressed if the rich possibilities of the different paradigms are to be realized in practice.

The functionalist contribution

The functionalist paradigm has provided the foundation for most modern theory and research on the subject of organization. For those committed to its underlying assumption, which in effect treat organization as an aspect of a wider societal system that serves the interests of its members, the paradigm has been spectacularly successful. It is seen as providing the basis for an organization and management theory that contributes to the progress and development of the wiser society. Organization theorists and researchers are seen from this point of view as making substantive and helpful contributions to the development of our organizational society.

While it is recognized that this mode of organizational research may in practice serve to enhance one set of individual or societal values as opposed to another, or one set of interests as opposed to another, this is seen as involving a problem of its use rather than of its fundamental nature. Functionalist theory is seen in principle as being able to serve management, workers, government, interorganizational networks or any client's perspective, according to the orientation of its user. The perspective generates theories, techniques, and detailed research findings that claim to contribute to our knowledge about the empirical nature of organization, and encourage us to see the role of values as a separate variable in the research process.

Specifically, it is possible to identify a number of major contributions to which functionalist organization theory can lay claim. Though functionalist theorists do not often list them in the way shown below, the listing does in fact capture the essential contribution which they make.

Functionalist organization theory creates and elaborates a 'language' for the management and control of organizations

Functionalist theory has typically viewed organization as a problematic phenomenon, and has seen the problem of organization as synonymous with the problem of 'efficiency' and, more recently, of 'effectiveness'. Theory and research has sought to generate useful perspectives, models, metaphors, concepts and detailed research findings which help to structure and control organized activity in pursuit of system states deemed efficient and effective. Taylorism, Human Relations, Theory X, Y, X, concepts of structure, technology, environment, etc., all share this common property. They attempt to create and systemize a language of organizational life that helps to structure organizational reality in a way that makes controlled performance possible. Modern organization and management theory constitutes a language of control which has evolved in nature and sophistication to cope with changing requirements of organizational control.

New theories - networks of concepts and relationships - are offered as new languages for structuring organizational life, and in many cases have been adopted in the actual management of organization theory can lay claim to great practical success, for it provides a direct means of structuring organization as a practical activity.

Functionalist organization theory provides its clientele with a 'mirror' through which it can see and assess itself

In addition to creating new languages for organization, functionalist theory has borrowed heavily from existing organizational language as a means of structuring and understanding organizational reality. To this extent, organization theorists engage in an act of unwitting collusion with the ideas and actions of those they attempt to study, articulating and refining theories in use. Much of classical management theory is of this kind, codifying practices in terms of general principles. Such codification performs a 'mirroring' function against which clients, for example managers, can reflect on and assess their current practice.

The codified theories in use provide clients with an opportunity to affirm or negate and change their practice. It allows them to see and assess more clearly exactly what they are doing. Much discussion on management courses involves the use of theory as a mirror, and of course, is about the appropriateness of new as against existing languages of organization. In the mirroring function, as in the creation of new language, much modern organization theory can claim spectacular success, as witnessed by the marketability of its ideas to client groups, particularly organizational managers.

Functionalist organization theory generates problem-solving ideas and practices designed to enhance the adaptive capacity of organization as a continuing process

The 'problems' which a functionalist theorist sees in an organizational context usually hinge upon the perception of some form of breakdown in the control of ordered activity. An inefficiency in management procedure, a conflict between superior and subordinate, or some form of withdrawal from work as in the case of an employee strike, may be defined and recognized as problems. In each case the functionalist theorist seeks to find ways in which these problems can be overcome, and ordered operation restored. Much of the theory and practice of organizational development (OD), for example, is devoted to this activity.

Somewhat paradoxically, the change orientation which characterizes OD is in point of fact geared towards the creation of a continuity of process. The tensions which underlie the 'problem', if left to themselves, may lead to disruptive changes in the system, perhaps of a qualitative kind. The 'problem-solving' solutions of the OD change consultants will usually contribute to the emergence of new forms of order bases on a new-found or newly developed adaptive capacity. In this sense, organizational change agents often work to preserve the status quo, not in the sense of creating stability, but in the sense of fostering homeostasis. The same is true of organization theorists concerned with the adaption of an organization to its environment through the development of strategy-structure relationships that preserve the organization as a successful, evolved member of an existing species, The functional study of power and politics often serves the same ends, yielding insights which help to make political activity manageable, often by making managers better politicians.

The status quo orientation of functionalist theory must in point of fact be regarded as its *raison d'etre,* and one of its major strengths. Functionalist organization theory in essence actively strives to create adaptability and organized change to minimize and counteract the possibility of more extreme forms of disruptive disjunctural change.

Functionalist organization theory attempts to generate generalizable knowledge that can be regarded as valid and reliable

Drawing inspiration from achievements in the natural sciences, functionalist research seeks to discern the regularities and relationships that characterize the world of organization, in a way that renders them subject to prediction and control. The knowledge generated by the functionalist researcher thus serves the general regulative orientation of the underlying paradigm or world view which it expresses. Realistically, the knowledge thus generated provides a set of generalizable ideologies which can be used with some certainty for the management and control of organizations. Thus 'generalizable knowledge' on the relationships between job design and employee satisfaction, organization environment - effectiveness, etc., serves to provide guidelines for organizational action in different situations. The knowledge generated in effect creates or reinforces a system of belief for guiding action.

The equation here of knowledge and ideology is not intended as a specified criticism of the functionalist viewpoint. The knowledge generated by all paradigms must be regarded as ideological to the extent that there appear to be no independent reference points for determining validity. The particular strengths which the functionalist can claim for the knowledge he or she strives to obtain is that it is *internally* valid and reliable, generalizable to some degree, and hence useful as a basis for action. Usefulness is celebrated as a major criterion for judging the worth and legitimacy of knowledge.

Functionalist organization theory in effect attempts to create a world characterized by certainty

This contribution is in many respects a corollary of the four listed above. The whole thrust and direction of functionalist theory is towards the development of a cohesive system of thought, where everything has a place within a web of ordered relationships that are intelligible, predictable and controlled. Its quest is for a bedrock of knowledge and an armoury of technique through which human beings can manage and regulate their world in relatively clear-cut, systematic ways. It could be said that it is intellectual response to the experience of the uncertainty and ambiguity of the world, and provides much solace and comfort to those desiring such structure.

Interestingly, the way functionalist theory hinges on and responds to the problem of uncertainty is clearly reflected in many conceptions of the nature of organization. For example, classic works in organization theory such as March and Simon and Thompson characterize organization as a process of reducing uncertainty, and external environments are often characterized in terms of the uncertainty dimension. The functionalism logic of organization is bases on the idea that it is possible for humans to master and control contest and destiny Functionalist organization theory draws on and fosters this belief and contributes operative ideologies and technologies of organized action which can claim major short-run success in the creation of a world believed to be certain, real in nature and effect, and amenable to control.

The history of functionalism is of course, very short, and whether it will be able to claim success in the long run remains to be seen.

The interpretive contribution

The interpretive paradigm directly challenges the preoccupation with certainty that characterizes the functionalist perspective, showing that order in the social world, however real in surface appearance, rests on a precarious, socially-constructed web of symbolic relationships that are continuously negotiated, renegotiated, affirmed or changed. The interpretive theorist's problematic is to understand the meaning and significance of this web of relationships, and how it exists as such. The perspective, though often expressed in ways that seem opaque and geared to providing no more than an intellectual and purely destructive critique of all that is 'useful' in functionalist theory, does have many direct and important implications for understanding and managing organization.

An interpretive approach to organization theory suggests that we must understand 'certainty' and the quest for certainty as a socially constructed phenomenon, and that organization theorists and practitioners should confront this and the other myths and ideologies which underwrite their practice

For the interpretive theorist and researcher all human beings are in various degrees makers and believers of practical myths, through which they make sense of action and acquire coherence in their lives. The world of organization is seen and understood as a realm of activity characterized by particular forms of myth-making that express significant networks of rules or models of action and give form to contextually based systems of meaning. The realization that we construct organization symbolically generates a healthy respect for the tentativeness of its fundamental nature, and cautions the organization theorist, lay and academic, against excessive commitment to favoured conceptions of organizational reality.

The interpretive perspective suggests that we

treat our conception of organizational reality as a useful fiction which we use to guide our understanding of activities and events in this milieu. The perspective suggests that we should see and understand every person as his or her own personal theorist, living life in accordance with the dictates of the theories and explanations thus constructed. This view of organizational reality provides an injunction to organizational members to remember and own the role they play in the construction of their reality, and appreciate the power and control they have over their own situation. The perspective deconcretizes our view of organizational reality and suggests that we should not be held in awe by the practices and structures in which we find ourselves. This general insight has a number of specific implications for the understanding and conduct of organizational practice, as discussed below.

An interpretive view of organizational reality provides an impetus for innovation

When organizational members specifically realize that they guide their lives through means of fictions, the way is open for innovation through the creation of new fictions. Thus organizational members may specifically begin to see the same situation in different ways, juxtaposing insights to create new modes of organizational theory and practice. Though the systematic use of new metaphors of organization, new languages of organization can be developed in a coherent and systematic way and, equally important, the limitations and implications of existing languages more clearly appreciated.

An interpretive view of organizational reality sensitizes organizational members to the importance of understanding organization as a cultural phenomenon rich in contextually bases systems of meaning

An appreciation of organizational life from this perspective hinges on an appreciation of the shared meanings that permit organized activity to emerge and assume coherence as an ongoing social form. The management of organized activity in this view hinges on the successful management of meaning, and points to the importance of managers being fully aware and skilled in the use of various symbolic modes of discourse through which situationally significant patterns of meaning and attention can be created and changed. An understanding of the symbolic nature of organization also provides the basis for an epistemology of management bases on an appreciative wisdom that recognises organization as resting not simply on the manipulation of cause and effect relationships, so much as on the patterning of symbolic discourse. Symbols and their relationships, i.e. patterns of contextually based meaning, become a principal focus of attention.

Organizational practice is understood as a continuous process of enactment

Implicit in the points made above, the idea that organizational members enact their own reality deserves special mention as one of the clearest and most important implications of the interpretive perspective. For it stresses that although organizational reality may at times appear 'all too real', the realness is of a socially constructed kind. What is real in organizations ultimately depends on the human beings that sustain the realness. Even the brute force of assembly line technology, for example, depends ultimately on the decisions of human beings to work within such a system or, from a managerial or trade union point of view, to adhere to the technology on which such a system depends. Some situation may appear more real than others, but the realness is always the product of human agency. Reality as a consensually valid system of meaning is at best an intersubjective phenomenon, with different individuals enacting reality in a similar way. Interpretive theory points to the unwitting collusion that underwrites the realness of organizational structure, rules, roles, and virtually every feature of organizational life.

Organizational contexts are enacted domains

This particular kind of enactment deserves special emphasis, for among all organizational concepts, that of the environment is often seen as being most independent and real in its consequences for any given organization. Yet it is clear that environments are enacted social processes. The independence and robustness of an environment stems from the actions of significant actors that comprise and shape 'the environment'. The environment which an organization encounters is also a product of the past enactments of that organization, and in this sense, it is a dimension of its own action and behaviour, and to this extent is under a measure of direct control. Present and future are defined and inhabited by past decisions which often come to haunt organizations like ghosts from the past. By way of example, I take a vivid illustration relating to the US motor industry, which I owe to Bill Starbuck. The US motor industry views itself as occupying a stagnating environment which, apart from its failure to offset foreign competition through an earlier move to the production of smaller cars, is seen as independent of their own decisions, and certainly not of their own choosing. One wonders, however, what the motor industry would be like if it had evolved technologically as fast as the computer and information processing industry. On this score we might expect some change in the whole concept of transportation or, with some exaggeration, cars that travel somewhere close to the speed of light. The motor industry has not evolved technologically in this way, and the non-actions in this regard in part account for its current predicament. The whole thrust of the interpretive paradigm is to suggest that the world which we inhabit is much more of our own making than we are usually prepared to recognize.

The radical humanist contribution

The radical humanist paradigm is specifically concerned with studying the self laid traps which interpretive theory shows us the human beings are so adept at constructing. In essence, it is concerned with understanding the way humans construct a world which they often experience as confining and most importantly, with finding ways in which humans can exercise control over their own constructions that allow them to express and develop their nature as human beings. the critical edge which characterizes radical humanist thought derives from the view that social life should express rather than constrain our humanness. The perspective offers a number of potentially important contributions to an understanding of organizations.

The radical humanist perspective searches for the ideological traps and blinders that lead human beings to feel powerless in dealing with the contingencies of their everyday world

For many in organizations, the enacted world appears 'all too real'. Workers and managers alike often function as alienated automatons, claiming no influence or power over the actions in which they engage. The nature of organization and environment confronts the individual as imperative, guided by impersonal forces or even blind necessity. The individual stands apart from a world experienced as an objective reality. Much of this seeming objectivity stems from those processes through which humans have learned to attribute a false correctness to their milieux.

Workers and managers alike often experience the concepts through which they structure their world as real forces; they believe their reality to be real, rather than merely an extension of themselves, i.e. an objectification of their experience of the world. This feeling of false concreteness is, from the radical humanist standpoint, one of the great barriers to the development of a reflexive awareness of the interactive relationships between subject and object, i.e. of the process of enactment. Radical humanist critique of the alienation and false concreteness embedded in our use of language, ideology, etc., provided an important means of developing in individuals a power and responsibility for guiding their own actions. The perspective provides a means of regaining power over our social constructions, so that individuals can consciously attempt to make their organizational and everyday life, rather than experiencing that they are merely being made by it.

The radical humanist perspective draws attention to the power dimension underlying enactment processes

Some people's processes of enactment are more important than others, for by virtue of position or charismatic qualities, they may assume great influence over the sensemaking processes of others. Leadership roles, for example, are characterized by a process of power-bases reality construction in which certain individuals may perceive or are perceived to hold a right and obligation to define the reality of others. such situations enact a pattern of dependency relations in which leaders feel obliged to define situations, and others to engage in a kind of 'trained inaction', waiting upon the definition of others, i.e. 'to follow' and 'be led'. Radical humanism offers a critical understanding of such phenomena showing, for example, that the 'all too realness' of leadership is predicated in power that derives as much from the enactment of followership, as on the initiatives of the leader. Throughout the organization of social life, it is possible to discern institutionalized power relationships which sustain social forms constraining human development. Radical humanism serves, through critique of these forms, the democratic ideal of restoring power to people.

The radical humanist perspective reveals the ethical dimension embedded in systems of meaningful action

John Van Maanen notes in a consideration of the way radical humanist thought can enrich interpretive theory, that meanings are ultimately practical, in essence provide solutions to the problems of existence. Different systems of meaning offer different kinds of solutions, and have different consequences. Viewed in this way, it becomes clear that configurations of meaning have an ethical or moral dimension amenable to both discussion and critique. Radical humanist thought presents an approach for understanding and confronting the moral codes which underwrite modes of organizational life, posing organizational choice as much a problem of moral principle as it is of technique.

Radical humanism highlights the unconscious significance of organization

One of the most important but often neglected aspects of radical humanist though focuses on the role of the unconscious mind in shaping the world of everyday activity. Organizations from this point of view are rich in symbolic significance, and many organizational events and activities are to be understood as manifestations of deep psychic processes that are at best poorly understood. An appreciation of the deep psychological significance of various aspects of organizational practices generates important insights on the paradoxes and double-binds underlying the enactment of organizational realities that make effective action difficult, if not impossible.

Radical humanism advocates an ideology which places people first

Organization is seen as being ultimately for people rather than the other way around. Whereas most theories of organizations view human beings as either tools or resources to be used for the purpose of organization, radical humanism stresses that organization should express our humanness and its potentialities. In this way, radical humanism sets the foundations of a truly humanistic vision for the practice of organized activity.

The radical structuralist contribution

Of all the paradigms, the radical structuralist is perhaps among the most misunderstood, particularly because of its roots in Marxist theory and the popular but misguided view that Marxism constitutes no more than a set of belief as to what society should be like. In point of fact, Marxist theory presents a rigorous mode of social analysis which generates insights of a distinctive kind. In judging the merits of this mode of analysis, it is largely irrelevant as to whether one believes in capitalism, socialism, communism or whether any other mode of organization constitutes an ideal kind. The important point is that its mode of analysis leads us to see social phenomena in ways that elude the perspectives characteristic of other paradigms, and which have major relevance for understanding modern organization.

The radical structuralist perspective provides us with a theory of organization which emphasizes the importance of self-generated change

Most traditional explanations of social change draw in one way or another upon casual models which look to external factors as a means of understanding how change as a phenomenon is shaped. The radical structuralist view, on the other hand, is premised on the dialectical notion that everything changes itself as a result of the tensions which its very existence creates, All organized forms, for example, are negated by what they are not. Any act of management, for example, immediately sets up a dialectical tension between itself and the managed situation which it has created. The managed situation stands in opposition to the act of management. Although this force for change may appear to be externally generated, in point of fact it emerges as a direct consequence of the original action. All organized forms can be seen as embodying this characteristic, which sets the basis for their own transformation. The implications of understanding change from this point of view are enormous, and provide the basis for a dialectical theory of management which recognizes the negational consequences of its own action.

Radical structuralist theory focuses on the generative mechanisms that characterize the deep structure of a mode of organization, to reveal its fundamental logics of action

The dialectical processes referred to above produce a world amenable to empirical observation which is of awesome complexity. The radical structuralist maintains that beneath the clutter of facts and observations which characterize this empirical world it is possible to discern generative mechanisms that provide important structural explanations of the whole. In other words, radical structuralist analysis discerns logics of action within social systems that provide unique insights on and explanations of the nature of the surface phenomena that characterize the empirical world. This perspective offers a mode of organizational analysis that allows us to identify the major dialectical oppositions that shape our culture. It can be argued that this has direct consequences for the entropic system tendencies which underlie the turbulence of our organizational society, and has direct implications for the formulation of governmental and corporate strategy.

The radical structuralist perspective encourages an understanding of the role organizations play in the total social formation in which they are set

Organizations, from this point of view, are empirical facets of an underlying mode of organization, and their nature and significance can only be understood in terms of the role they play within the whole. Radical structuralist analysis encourages a perspective on organization which has considerable relevance for understanding the role of the state, and the distinctions between various kinds of public and private institutions. For example, it offers a specific view on the nature of regulative agencies, suggesting that we understand their role in terms of the under-lying contradictions in the mode of social organization which has produced them. This mode of analysis has direct relevance for the formation of public policy, particularly in the late twentieth century, an era when policies on regulation and deregulation swing like a political pendulum, in ignorance of the role and function of regulation in mediation of contradictions.

The radical structuralist perspective offers a distinctive understanding of organizations in crisis

Crisis is of special interest to the radical structuralist, because in such situations it is often possible to discern the workings of social system much more clearly than in those periods of surface stability when potentially contradictory elements are 'overdetermined' and in a state of temporary balance. The approach of the radical structuralist is to understand crises in terms of the logic of the whole social system, and to draw distinctions between the crises that are functional for maintenance of the whole against those which herald major transformations of the whole. Here again these insights have direct implications for the way we respond to and handle organizational crises.

The radical structuralist perspective offers a conception of organization as a form of praxis concerned with the self-transformation of collective action

Organizational praxis is not so much concerned with instrumental, practical problem-solving of a social engineering kind, such as that associated with usual discussions on the nature of innovation, as with the development of a capacity for self-organization which allows transcendence of existing constraints embedded in subject and object worlds. Praxis constitutes a form of action which seeks to transform itself through its interaction with the object world. As an example, we can point to the collective self-transformation which appears to be taking place in late twentieth century. Poland, where trade unions are attempting to transform their situation, not in a piecemeal fashion, but through action designed to create a new social form. An understanding of this process, whereby new social forms emerge from contradictions in the old, provides the basis for a new way of conceptualizing and facilitating the process of social innovation in the widest sense.

Harnessing new opportunities for organizational research

Throughout the above discussion, emphasis has been placed on identifying the contributions which different paradigms can make to our understanding of organization. This approach has been adopted to move debate about paradigms beyond recognition that different perspectives exist, to a stage at which we can begin to harness the possibilities which they offer. If the chapter has made its case effectively, there can be no doubt at all that the paradigms are worthy of investigation for organizational analysis. Each paradigm offers important insight which eludes other perspectives, and while the implications of the contradictory nature of many of the assumptions on which they are bases must ultimately addressed much can be done to advance organizational analysis immediately by attempting to realize the rich possibilities they offer. Organizational analysis, interpreted in the widest sense to incorporate the usual distinctions between organizational behaviour,theory, development, policy, etc., should grasp the opportunity and challenge which paradigm diversity presents, and explore the new perspectives which are available.

In order for this to be achieved in practice, attention needs to be given to the barriers posed by number of institutional constraints associated with the way scientific enquiry is presently organized. There are a number of factors which serve to encourage organization researchers, particularly those who are just embarking on their academic careers, to engage in research which is 'safe' to the extent that it builds on past achievements in different subject areas and presents little challenge to the status quo. In line with the constructive nature and intent of this chapter as whole, it will be useful to discuss the constraints in terms of the challenges which they present. I will confine attention to just three.

There is a need to develop a greater sensitivity for the practice and requirements of intellectual craftsmanship

Much conduct of organizational research, and the training of researchers of contemporary graduate programmes, is dominated by the requirements of methodology or technique. It is perhaps an exaggeration to suggest that organizational research is driven by methods searching for problems and situations to be researched, but it makes the fundamental point. In comparison with the attention given to methodology, the need for researchers to become familiar with and understand the multifaceted nature of the phenomenon being studied us given relatively little attention. It is in this sense that there is a need for a greater sense of intellectual craftsmanship.

A craftsperson, whether engaged in creative or relatively functional work, cannot perform effectively simply by knowing his or her tools. Craftsmanship also depends on an understanding of the material being worked. For organizational researchers, this material is found in the phenomenon of organization, and an understanding of this material depends on careful examination and experience of the phenomenon. An understanding of the way we can constitute the phenomenon in different ways on the basis of different paradigms provides one means through which we can make sense of our experience of the phenomenon. An understanding of the intellectual traditions which define these paradigms provides us with access to the thoughts and insights of the great theorists who have recorded their experience of social organization from these different standpoints.

The notion of paradigm can thus be used as a tool for exploring the nature of the phenomenon that we are concerned to investigate. Even though a researcher may eventually decide to conduct research from the perspective of one given paradigm, an exploration of the nature of other paradigms provides an invaluable basis for understanding what one is doing, and why other alternatives are to be rejected. An understanding of the different paradigms also opens up the possibility of engaging in dialectical modes of research which attempt to counterpose the insights generated from competing perspectives.

There is a need to develop and refine the strategies and tools of research appropriate to different paradigms, and to develop appropriate criteria for determining the quality of the research conducted

There is a need for methodological innovation, and in particular for consideration of the logics of research practice characteristic of different paradigms. There is a special need to develop understanding of the vital link between theory and method in social research, and to appreciate the way sound research practice must be true to the logic of the assumptions which underwrite that practice.

Steps in this direction were taken in a research methodology project which counterposed the logics of twenty different kinds of research practice, and assessed the nature of their competing insights. This approach offered the possibility of replacing debates about the merits of competing methodologies with a consideration of the merits of rival logics of research. It offered the possibility of opening a new frontier of debate; one which assesses the significance of research strategies from the perspectives of different paradigms rather than from strategies from the perspectives of different paradigms rather than from the traditional standpoint of a simple correspondence theory of truth.

There is need to justify the institutional constraints imposed by academic journals and university departments on research practice, to facilitate the innovation and risk-taking necessary to explore unconventional research perspectives

One of the most frequent responses to the suggestion that there is a need for exploration of different paradigms in organizational research is that those who do so will fail to 'get published', and fail to 'get tenure'. At a recent *Academy of Management* doctoral consortium, numerous doctoral students responded to a debate on paradigms for organizational research with the view that they felt there was little room for innovation in their doctoral work, since only conventional research activities were appreciated and rewarded. In other words, there are signs of a well spread feeling in many academic departments that there are few practical alternatives to orthodoxy, even among those newcomers to organizational research who might be expected to relish the challenge of a new opportunity. The control systems developed by journals and university departments alike exert a confining if well-meaning hold on the jugular of scholarship, which threatens to strangle the development of new possibilities. The existence of paradigm diversity thus present a special challenge to those who control sources of publication, and to those who administer research opportunities through control of funding and careers. At a minimum, it is a challenge to become proactive in encouraging the pursuit of new endeavour, and to be tolerant, helpful and understanding toward those who are sufficiently inquisitive and courageous to explore the new research frontiers which are in such obvious need of attention.

Index